NOW YOU CAN MAKE DISCIPLES!

A Step-By-Step Guide

Mike Falkenstine

Rick & Abbie,
Appreciate you guys!
Enjoy the new book!
Mt. 28:18-20,
Mike Falkenstine

ONE:EIGHT
CATALYST
RESOURCE

Now You Can Make Disciples!
A Step-By-Step Guide

Copyright 2022 by Mike Falkenstine

Published by One Eight Catalyst, P.O. Box 630336, Littleton, CO 80163

www.OneEightCatalyst.org

Unless otherwise noted, all Scripture quotation are from The Holy Bible, English Standard Version. ESV® Text Edition: 2016. Copyright © 2001 by Crossway Bibles, a publishing ministry of Good News Publishers.

Additional copies of this book can be found on Amazon.com

The author would be happy to communicate with you about any questions, comments or suggestions you may have. Please follow Mike on Twitter and Facebook at MikeonMission.

ISBN: 978-1-7336283-5-8

Table of Contents

Acknowledgments

There are so many who contributed toward my own spiritual formation and growth, that I cannot mention them all, nor can I mention all the people who have enabled me to write this book. I would like to try to acknowledge some key people:

I want to give all the glory, honor and praise to God the Father and His Son, Jesus Christ. Psalm 115:1

To my wife Sherie, a formidable disciple maker in her own right. Love you, sweetie!

To the Wednesday morning Bible Study guys, who are so faithful to come and allow me to teach them the next thing God has been showing me. Thank you Ron, Lonny and Mike.

To the proofreaders who made such wonderful suggestions and reminders of things that I knew but had forgotten. Thank you Brian, Steve and Brad.

To the partners and friends of One Eight Catalyst, thank you all so much for allowing me to pursue God's direction and see it come to fruition.

And finally, to Brad Miller, the Navigator staff who first discipled me as a wayward 22 year old. Appreciate you dear brother!

Introduction

The genesis for this new book has been a long time in the making. When I first went on staff with The Navigators in 1994, I quickly began to speak about disciple making and discipleship in Sunday morning services, Sunday School classes and the occasional ministry benefit events. It was clear by the looks on people's faces, and by their reaction after the speaking time was completed, that while they were happy that God had called me to commit my life to the cause of making disciples that make disciples, the command that Jesus gave to all Christians to "Go therefore and make disciples of all nations, baptizing them in the name of the Father and of the Son and of the Holy Spirit, teaching them to observe all that I have commanded you. And behold, I am with you always, to the end of the age"[1] was not directed towards or meant for them to obey. Seemingly in their mind, that command was only for those who have been called, like me, toward full-time Christian service.

For years now, this has left me perplexed. As Christians, we believe that the Bible is the inspired Word of God, and that it's reliable because of its authority. We also know that Jesus, who is our Lord and Savior, has full authority in our lives as we've surrendered ourselves to Him.[2] So it would stand to reason that if Jesus, as recorded in the Bible, gave us a direct command to 'Go and make disciples,' that we would immediately snap to

1. Matthew 28:19-20
2. Luke 9:23-25

attention and say, 'Yes sir, on the job sir!' And yet, even though I spend a lot of time with people who are active in their churches and who clearly love Jesus, very few of them, dare I say almost none of them, know how to go through the process of helping another Christian grow in their walk with Jesus in a way that would enable that Christian to reproduce what they've learned into the life of another.

Although I've spent the majority of the 28 years I've been in full-time ministry serving the growth of the Church in China, I've always had people who I've invested in their spiritual formation. In 2016, I felt a strong calling to create resources and deliver training that is helping Christians grow spiritually in order to help them reach their world for Christ. In this work I'm doing now with One Eight Catalyst,[3] which is the ministry I now direct, I have a typical talk I give as I promote the mission and vision of One Eight Catalyst. In this talk, I lay out the three passages of Scripture I use to compose my definition of the Great Commission, and I end this section of my talk with quoting one of two passages in John 14. It is these passages in John 14 that really tie it all together because after we read about the commands of the Great Commission that Jesus gives to all Christians, He states in John 14:15 that "whoever has my commands and obeys them, he it is who loves me." What follows is really astonishing to me: Complete and total blank looks from the congregation! It's as if they are saying, 'Mike, I understand that the passages you quoted are in the Bible and that Jesus is the one who gave the commands, but I wouldn't know how to make a disciple if my life depended on it!' There are many reasons for those blank looks, which I won't cover here in great detail since I've already covered that in my book *Being and Making Disciples in the Western Church: A First Steps Guide,*[4] but I think it's safe to say that both in individuals lives

3. OneEightCatalyst.org
4. Digital Copy is available at no cost at OneEightCatalyst.org

and in our churches, we don't have enough emphasis on the importance of each Christian being able to make disciples that make disciples.

Some of the most exciting things that God is currently doing in the One Eight Catalyst ministry is both the requests we regularly get to translate our book resources into languages around the world and the chance to teach some of our key content worldwide. As a part of these projects, I was recently in Kenya teaching 100 pastors content from my book on the six marks of a disciple of Jesus. Toward the end of this training just outside of Nairobi, the Pastor who invited me asked if I could take a couple of hours after the Sunday worship time to be able to teach these pastors a 'step by step' process on how to actually make disciples. The Pastor is seminary trained, but no one had taught him or any of the 100 pastors on the steps required in order to make disciples that make disciples. I happily obliged, having carefully studied, catalogued, and memorized the basic steps of discipleship years ago. That additional training session was a real success, and it was the third time in two years that either a Christian pastor or leader had asked me to help them know how to make disciples that make disciples.

It's clear to me that both at home and abroad, there is a critical need for Christians to know how to make disciples, and because I have a deep heart to create resources that help Christians grow spiritually, enabling them to reach their world for Christ, I present this new book resource. In writing this book, I pray that it would become the ultimate resource for those who want to obey Jesus' commands to make disciples as a step-by-step guide on how you can help another Christian grow in their walk with Jesus, to the point they can do the same things with someone else. In other words, if you don't know how to make disciples and you want to know how to make disciples, this book is for you. The multiplication principles of discipleship can have deep and meaningful effects. Let me illustrate that for you. Let's say that you began meeting with someone this year and begin to help them become a fully devoted follower of Jesus, and next year, you and this other person each began meeting with a new person in discipleship, at the end of next year, you'd have four people that are equipped to disciple others. At the beginning of year 3, if the four of you each got a new person and met in a discipleship relationship, you'd have 8 people by the end of the year. If this pattern continued year after year, where those that had been discipling and discipled each got a new person to disciple the next year, it would only take you 31 years to reach and disciple all 7.9 billion people on earth! Of course, we know that the multiplication principle would eventually break down, but the point is still valid: You can have a huge impact by only meeting with one person a year, with the heart that you're teaching them to be able to teach others.

While acknowledging Paul's intent in 2 Timothy 2 as he writes, "and what you have heard from me in the presence of many witnesses entrust to faithful men, who will be able to teach others also", I know I'm not going to be able to disciple you through these pages. I do think there is a 'back door' to accomplishing my task here in that if this book is thorough enough to walk you through each step and easy enough to accomplish, with easy to follow instruction and examples from my own disciple making journey, I truly believe that you can become a maker of disciples where you weren't before you started reading and using this book. My other main hope and challenge in writing this book is that there is already a wonderful book resource on this topic that so many have used in the journey of becoming a disciple maker. Leroy Eims, former Navigator staff member wrote the 1978 classic, *The Lost Art of Disciple Making.*[5] This book was formative for me when I was first coming along as a young Navigator staff member, and if you were able to see my personal copy, you could tell that it has been well used. Reading through it again, I fell in love all over again with how well researched and written it is, but I was left with the thought that a newer book was needed in this area. Mr. Eims' book was written in 1978, with no revisions or newer editions, and while the Scriptural truths and many of the processes in the book will never change, much of the 'how to' is a bit different, both because our culture has changed quite a bit since 1978, and the volume of electronic and web-based tools has improved since then. My greatest hope would be, like a new edition of a well translated Bible, to build on the foundation of Mr. Eims' work and provide you with a fresh volume to enable you to make disciples that make disciples.

So, here's what I'd like to do for the remainder in the Introduction of this book. Let me first give a brief overview of what you'll find in this book, then in Chapter 1 I'll want to define some terms that I'll be using throughout this volume since defining terms will help us all be 'on the same page' of what I'm talking about when the terms are used. Because there is a lot involved with the making of disciples, I'm going to try my best to use my powers of summarizing, while still giving you the essentials. In this book, we'll look first at what is a disciple and what are the basics of disciple making. We'll also look at why it's important for us all to be disciple makers. Before we can begin, there is some preparation that needs to take place, including shoring up trouble areas in your own walk with Christ, since you can't give to someone something you don't have. After looking at why I often say that disciple making is an intentional process,

---

5. Eims, Leroy. 1978. The Lost Art of Disciple Making. Zondervan

we'll look at the disciplines of a disciple maker, which are disciplines that you as a disciple must know and must be practicing. Next, we look at the tools of a disciple maker, which is one of the things that has changed quite a bit since 1978. These tools are important; we'll look at why they are important and how you can and should use them.

Once you understand the disciplines and tools of a disciple maker, we begin the process of asking someone if they would pray about meeting with you one-on-one with the intent of you helping them to grow spiritually. This is a big step, since many Christians I know don't feel like they have much to give to another Christian, but once you understand who you are in Christ, what He's done in your life and you have the disciplines and tools, you'll be ready. We'll look at how exactly you can ask someone to begin meeting, what that 'ask' looks like, and why I think this should be a very intentional and thorough process. There's also the issue here of asking the 'right' person, and how you can make mistakes in asking the 'wrong' person,' and I'll show you how to discern the difference. You then have found the 'right' person and it's time to begin meeting together. Now what? There are more than a few things you'll want to be looking for here: While you begin meeting with this person, of course you'll want to be building a good relationship together, but you'll also want to be intentional about the purpose of why you all have started meeting together. I'll help you see the balance there between being relational and intentional in your times together. This meeting together is also a 'life on life' process where you're sharing your life with them, even as they are doing the same with you. And what should these meetings look like? What are you actually doing during that time? I can provide for you a template for those times and as you get more experience, you can develop your own template based on what works for you in a way that objectives are accomplished. As you're meeting together, how do you know if the person you are discipling is growing? There are some guideposts I can provide.

As you begin meeting together, it's almost a guarantee that you'll run into some obstacles in the disciple making process. It can be hard to discern how to recognize them, what to do with those obstacles, and the seriousness of these obstacles. I'll help you navigate these obstacles, and how to make course corrections along the way. There are also certain people that you should not try to disciple, either because of a lack of motivation or because they're just not ready to grow in Christ in the way they should. We see both Jesus and the apostle Paul speak into this truth. We're all familiar with the Parable of the Sower that we see in Matthew 13, and some people's seed falls into rocky soil that's not able to grow and some has fallen in the good soil, and they are ready to grow. As you meet together with another in a discipleship relationship, you're going to want to have your 'antennas up' for both how to tell what spiritual growth looks like and when then it's time to begin encouraging those you are meeting with to begin praying about them investing their lives into the lives of another just like you have with them. This is what I call the 2 Timothy 2:2 principle, as Paul encourages the young Timothy to 'and the things you've heard me say...' Clearly, Paul didn't want his time, investment in life-on-life and his teaching to stop with Timothy. There would be a time Timothy would entrust Paul's teaching through life-on-life ministry and teaching with other people, who would be able to teach others also. We'll look at depth into the principle, but clearly Biblically we should always be keeping in mind that our investment of time should be looked at not only from the lens of the person we're meeting with, but also in a way that person can be entrusting these things to others. In a principle I call 'off boarding,' there will be a time where you'll want the person you've been meeting with to spend more of their time investing in others, and you'll move to an 'advisory' roll with them as they need you to speak into their own questions or obstacles they are finding as they are meeting with others.

Final Encouragement

Many people I talk to about learning how to obey Jesus' command for us all to be making disciples show great angst and uncertainty about their ability to actually help another Christian grow spiritually. They don't believe they have anything to share with another Christian and that this 'making disciples' business is for the professionals, people like me or their pastor. The problem with this line of thinking is that obeying Christ is not only for the 'professionals.' Obeying Christ is for us all, and He's calling us all to 'Go and make disciples.' So, let's get serious about learning what that means and how to do it. My encouragement to you is the same encouragement that Paul had for the church at Rome, "I myself am satisfied about you, my brothers, (literally brothers and sisters) that you yourselves are full of goodness, filled with all knowledge and able to instruct one another."[6] If you've accepted Christ and you are full of the Holy Spirit, I'm satisfied that you have something to share and you are able to instruct others.

Let's go!

---

6. Romans 15:14

Chapter 1

The Basics of Disciple Making

I'm not ashamed to admit that I love a good story. Whether in a good book or movie, or even a television show that I'm interested in watching, I am quick to notice whether the story is well written or not. And I think, even unconsciously, most of us pick up on whether the story is well written, since entertainment that has a well written story is usually a lot more successful than stories that are not well written. In my opinion, the story drives the whole ship in the entertainment industry! Of course, you want the acting to be good, but good actors with a bad story still make a bad television show or movie. Some of my favorite stories include a 'hidden in plain sight' element to the story because it can make the story super interesting. People's perceptions are revealed and challenged as these types of stories unfold. And since we all have our perceptions, that is, how we interpret, organize, and maintain the information we bring into our minds throughout the course of each day, many times these types of stories make us think deeper about how our own perception is filtered, sometimes erroneously. Whether it's the spy who is 'unseen' but is still out in public doing their work, the member of a community who is marginalized or intentionally unseen and comes to be seen, or the double crosser who seems like the protagonist but is really the antagonist, I love these types of stories.

I guess since I'm always on the lookout for a good 'hidden in plain sight' story, I am keenly aware of this happening in our Christian circles today. From the early days of my faith 36 years ago when I first became a Christian until today, there are a couple of biblical concepts that seem to be 'hidden in plain sight' because they are rarely talked or taught about in our churches today. I'm referring to the concepts of God's desire for us to be fully devoted disciples of Jesus and that He wants every one of us to be making disciples of Jesus is a story that while not completely hidden, since it only takes a Christian to do a thorough reading of the New Testament to see these concepts clearly, is 'hidden in plain sight.' While there are many reasons that I believe this is true, much of which I examined in detail in my book Being and Making Disciples in the Western Church: A First Steps Guide, I'd love to 'set the stage' for this book by showing you why I believe that we each need to be a disciple maker before I begin to walk you through the process of how to be able to help another Christian in their spiritual formation. But first, it would be imperative to define some terms here so that we're all on the same page.

Definition of Terms

If you've made it this far into my book, and you're not too 'freaked out' and you're still reading, I'm really glad. Let me say something at this point: It may seem super overwhelming to read through the full process of how to make disciples that I outlined in the Introduction, but let me assure you that you can do it, and you should attempt to do it because as we'll see in this chapter, Jesus really wants you to do it. And any time our Lord and Savior wants us to do something, we should try our best to do the thing He wants us to do. I promise you that going through this book step by step, learning the stages and steps of how to make disciples will be worth it, and God will bless your effort. Just as Isaiah writes, "How beautiful upon the mountains are the feet of him who brings good news, who publishes peace, who brings good news of happiness, who publishes salvation, who says to Zion, Your God reigns,"[1] by investing in the lives of others spiritual health, you too are bringing the good news that a life lived for Jesus will worth everything, your efforts are beautiful in God's sight. Here are four terms that you'll see a lot in this book:

Disciple

A disciple of Jesus is one who has accepted Christ as their Lord and Savior, becoming a new creation,[2] and adopted into the family of God as God's child,[3] 'sanctified' and washed clean,[4] given eternal life with God,[5] and whose citizenship for all eternity got a change in location![6] As we see clearly in Scripture, God never intended for us to receive Jesus as Savior, then go back to whatever we were doing in our own pursuits. Jesus wants us to be imitators of Him, to learn from Him and to follow Him. He wants us to be His disciples. A disciple of Jesus is someone who learns from Jesus how to live like Jesus — someone who, because of God's awakening grace, conforms his or her words and ways to the words and ways of Jesus. A disciple of Jesus wants to learn from Him, through the study of God's Word, the Bible, and as we listen to others teach from it. We make the Bible part of your life every day. As the Psalmist said, "With my lips I declare all the rules of your mouth."[7]

I always feel compelled in this discussion to distinguish the difference between a Christian and a disciple. A Christian is someone who has trusted Christ for forgiveness of sin and been assured of life forever

---

1. Isaiah 52:7
2. 2 Corthinians 5:17
3. Galatians 4:5
4. 1 Corinthians 6:11
5. John 10:28
6. Ephesians 2:19
7. Psalm 119:13

with Jesus. A disciple is someone who not only meets the above definition
of a Christian but is also following Jesus in an effort to learn how to
become more like him. In the early church, those that accepted Christ were
just called disciples.

Discipleship

Over the years, I've worked hard on my definition of discipleship,
because I think it's important. My longstanding definition of discipleship
has been meticulously crafted: Discipleship is the process by which a
Christian **with a life worth reproducing** commits himself for an extended
period of time to a few individuals who have trusted Christ, the purpose
being to aid and guide their growth to maturity and equip them to
reproduce themselves in a third spiritual generation. Let me highlight a
couple of key points here: Discipleship is undertaken by a Christian with a
life worth reproducing, which is an important point. As we'll see in more
detail in Chapter 2, you can't give to someone something you don't have,
and it's important to note that your walk with Christ, your undertaking of
spiritual disciplines that enable you to have a vibrant walk with Jesus must
be firmly in place before you attempt to help someone else grow spiritually.
Also, please note that discipleship is undertaken for an extended period of
time, meaning you can't really disciple another person as a part of a 8-week
church program. Discipleship at its core involves a life-on-life relationship
over an extended period, and I'll help you know what to do over that
extended period and when to know when to stop meeting together. And
finally, you see the aforementioned 2 Timothy 2:2 come through in my
definition, that the purpose of this extended period of meeting with
another who has been won to Christ is that they then will be able to do the

same thing with a third spiritual generation, that it would go from you to them, and them to others.

Disciple Making

Disciple making then is the actual 'how-to,' the making of disciples in the discipleship process, which is what this book is about. I'm often reminded that disciple making always starts with evangelism, since we can't have people to disciple without new believers! Once we have these new believers, there is a lot that goes into making disciples, but it's the process of taking a Christian who was not considered to be a disciple and helping them grow in their walk with Jesus so they are now disciples. This is important because it was always God's plan for those who accepted Christ to become disciples, and not just Christians. For example, as the apostle Paul was starting His ministry, he was seeking to make disciples. In the book of Acts, after a disturbance and attempted stoning in Iconium, we see Paul and Barnabas' focus in ministry in Derbe was not to make converts, but disciples: 'When they had preached the gospel to that city and had made many disciples.'[8] The goal of evangelism has always been to make disciples (not merely Christians), not only in the early church, but also today as we see Jesus command to us to "Go therefore and make disciples of all nations…."[9]

Spiritual Disciplines

In his excellent book, Spiritual Disciplines for the Christian Life,[10] Donald Whitney defines spiritual disciples as "those practices found in Scripture that promote spiritual growth among believers in the gospel of Jesus Christ. They are the habits of devotion and experiential Christianity

8. Acts 14.21
9. Matthew 28:19
10. Donald S. Whitney, Spiritual Disciplines for the Christian Life (Nav Press: Colorado Springs, 2014) p. 4

that have been practiced by the people of God since Biblical Times." In the resources section of this book, I have a list of the top spiritual disciplines and a short summary of how to implement them. They include everything from Reading God's word, Time in Prayer, Fasting, Scripture memory, Worship, Journaling and much more. They are practices a disciple of Jesus implements into their daily life in order to grow deeper in God and deeper intimacy in Christ.

Spiritual Formation

Spiritual Formation is the process of transformation of the disciple of Jesus, that their inmost desires form in such a way that the natural expression of their lives tilts toward the deeds of Christ done in the power of Christ. We see this play out in Scripture in a few ways. In Peter's second letter to the churches in Asia Minor he is writing about how the divine power of Christ can transform our lives, "His divine power has granted to us all things that pertain to life and godliness, through the knowledge of him who called us to his own glory and excellence, by which he has granted to us his precious and very great promises, so that through them you may become partakers of the divine nature, having escaped from the corruption that is in the world because of sinful desire. For this very reason, make every effort to supplement your faith with virtue, and virtue with knowledge, and knowledge with self-control, and self-control with steadfastness, and steadfastness with godliness, and godliness with brotherly affection, and brotherly affection with love."[11] We see the transformation of the disciple, growing and transforming into a fully devoted disciple of Jesus. Paul continues this idea in Romans 2, "Do not be conformed to this world, but be transformed by the renewal of your mind,

---

11. 2 Peter 1:4-7

that by testing you may discern what is the will of God, what is good and acceptable and perfect."[12] I love this passage because we can clearly see Paul's heart for those in the Roman church to be transformed from who they were before Christ into a disciple of Jesus who is pursuing both the will of God and that with the perfection we see in Jesus.[13]

What Discipleship is Not

It's important for me to give you a quick overview of what discipleship is not, since there are a lot of misconceptions about Discipleship and Disciple Making. Here are two things for you to consider when it comes to what Discipleship is not:

It's Not a Program

Over the years, I've found out that many church leaders believe discipleship to be a program, as church leaders will have an 8-week 'discipleship' program at their church and upon completion, the participants are 'discipled.' These programs focus on finishing the material given and after the program is over, discipleship has been completed. As I mentioned earlier, because discipleship is a life-on-life process over an extended period of time, it's impossible to create a discipleship program that would be effective or long lasting.

It's Not Just for Ministry Professionals

I believe that this is a big misperception in the Christian church today. For some, being a disciple maker is only for the ministry professionals, those who have committed their lives to full-time ministry and have received spiritual training. Instead, we should look at all of us as

---

12. Romans 12:2
13. Matthew 5:48

potential disciple makers, since we know Jesus calls us all to make disciples[14] and because we believe that God has authority over all things,[15] He wouldn't have His son ask us to do something that we couldn't ever do. If you have accepted Christ, you can do it![16]

On the other side of discipleship, I have heard a lot that having someone help you with your spiritual foundation in a discipleship relationship is only for new believers. Of course, new believers will greatly benefit from a discipleship relationship, but as we all know, our spiritual formation is a life-long pursuit. Just like the 10,000-hour rule that it takes 10,000 hours of intensive practice[17] to achieve mastery of anything, we could all use someone investing in our spiritual formation for the entirety of our lives. In my view, we don't have enough Christians practicing the basics of the Christian life, and as you'll see, investing in a discipleship relationship with another is great for your own spiritual formation.

What Does the Bible Say About Being and Making Disciples?

Let's continue by doing a little Bible Study together. We start with the calling of the first disciples of Jesus, as He speaks a simple command, "Follow me."[18] The word disciple, much like discipline, comes from the Latin word *discipulus,* meaning "pupil" or "learner." It refers to someone who adopts the ways of someone else. When applied to Jesus, a disciple is someone who learns from Jesus how to live like Jesus — someone who, because of God's awakening grace, conforms his or her words and ways to the words and ways of Jesus. The New Testament authors make this abundantly clear, both through recording the words of Jesus on this topic and through the letters written to the early church plants of Paul. Clearly, Jesus wanted his disciples to be about certain things, and following and

14. Matthew 28:19-20
15. Matthew 28:18
16. https://www.youtube.com/watch?v=qztuEucrNBc

17. Gladwell, Maxwell Outliers:The Story of Success (New York: Back Bay Books, 2016.)
18. Mark 1:17, 2:14, John 1:43

being with Him was at the top of that list. After His triumphal entry, Jesus stated, "If anyone serves me, **he must follow me; and where I am, there will my servant be also.** If anyone serves me, the Father will honor him."[19] Did you catch that? Not only are we as disciples of Jesus called to follow Him, but we're called to be where Jesus is. This requires that we put Jesus in the #1 spot in our lives. While dining at the house of a ruler of the Pharisees, Jesus makes this quite clear as He states, "If anyone comes to me and does not hate his own father and mother and wife and children and brothers and sisters, yes, and even his own life, he cannot be my disciple. Whoever does not bear his own cross and come after me cannot be my disciple."[20] While I don't believe Jesus is actually saying that we should literally hate our parents, since we know Jesus affirms the fifth commandment of Moses to "Honor your father and your mother", and, "Whoever reviles father or mother must surely die",[21] the implication here is clear: Jesus comes first, and if your parents and other family members reject Jesus and disown us as disciples of Jesus, we must follow Christ. Jesus is simply requiring us to prioritize our relationship with Jesus over our relationship with parents, siblings, and other family members. Jesus makes a similar statement in Luke 14 as he states, "any one of you who does not renounce all that he has cannot be my disciple."[22]

Another key attribute of a disciple of Jesus that I've focused on a lot in my own walk with Jesus over the last few years is a disciple of Jesus abiding in Christ. I've enjoyed my study of the word abide, which in Greek is menó, means 'to remain or stay in,' and it's this study that has been so useful for me, especially given some of the statements Jesus makes to us as His followers for us to "Abide in me, and I in you. As the branch cannot bear fruit by itself, unless it abides in the vine, neither can you, unless you

19. John 12:26
20. Luke 14:26-27
21. Mark 7:10

22. Luke 14:33

abide in me. I am the vine; you are the branches. Whoever abides in me and I in him, he it is that bears much fruit, for apart from me you can do nothing."[23] Did you catch what Jesus is saying to us? Remain in me, stay close to me, and in doing so, you'll bear fruit for me, and without remaining close to me, you can do nothing. None of us want to do nothing of value for Him! Combine that with Jesus' statement in John 8 where He states, "If you abide in my word, you are truly my disciples, and you will know the truth, and the truth will set you free", and we get a clear sense that those that are disciples of Jesus have a daily close relationship with Him.

Characteristics of a Disciple of Jesus

In my extensive study on what it means to be a disciple of Jesus and given the ground we've already covered, let me give you three areas to be continually focusing on and striving toward in our pursuit to be a fully devoted disciple of Jesus.

1. A Disciple Listens to Jesus

One could never claim to be a disciple of a teacher without being ready to listen to that teacher. The world is full of teachers who are looking for followers and listeners! A disciple of Jesus listens to Him and when Jesus speaks, the disciple listens. The disciple clings to every word of the Master as if that word were bread for the hungry or water for the thirsty. When Jesus gathered together His disciples on the Mount of Transfiguration, God the Father spoke from heaven with a clear command: "This is my beloved Son, with whom I am well pleased; listen to him."[24] To be a Christian implies that you listen intently to Jesus. I think we could clearly say that it

---

23. John 15:4-5
24. Matthew 17:5

would be hard to be following and abiding in Jesus if we're not listening to Jesus, which is mostly done through time with Jesus in prayer and by reading the Bible. Jesus himself states that "If you abide in my word, you are truly my disciples, and you will know the truth, and the truth will set you free."[25] I've called the decision of whether to get time daily with God in prayer and in His word to be the most critical decision we'll make on a daily basis. Skipping that time with God leaves you less connected to God and without an opportunity to hear his 'still, small voice.'[26]

2. A Disciple Learns from Jesus

We must not only listen to Jesus. A disciple does not listen and then turn away as though the teacher's words had no impact. When Jesus calls His disciples, He instructs them to learn from Him as well as to listen. When they respond to His call, He says, "Take my yoke upon you, and learn from me, for I am gentle and lowly in heart, and you will find rest for your souls."[27] To be a disciple is to be a learner, and the words of Christ carry weight. For those who are fully devoted followers of Jesus, our greatest desire is learning from Christ and is foundational to all that we as disciples believe. Joyfully receiving the words of the Master is as vital as daily bread, the disciple meditates upon them day and night.[28] And how can we best receive these words? I've often recommended to people that a slow and steady reading (maybe a couple times through!) of the Gospels is a great way to start. As you read, make some notes as to what you are reading, paying attention to what He is commanding you to do.

---

25. John 8:31-32
26. 1 Kings 18:20-40; 19:12
27. Matthew 11:29
28. Psalm 1:2

3. A Disciple Obeys Jesus

No one may call himself a disciple of Jesus who is not willing to obey Him. The disciple will put into practice what he learns from time with Jesus. Because Jesus has proven Himself worthy, not obeying Him is not an option. There is a passage in Luke 6 that always resonates very powerfully to me. Jesus uses an analogy of building a house on either a weak or strong foundation, and then He states, "Why do you call me 'Lord, Lord,' and not do what I tell you? Everyone who comes to me and hears my words and does them, I will show you what he is like: he is like a man building a house, who dug deep and laid the foundation on the rock."[29] As I read this passage, I can almost hear Jesus' heart breaking a little… He's saying, 'You call me your Lord, and yet you don't do what I am commanding you to do. Why is that?' And as we'll see later in this chapter, Jesus gives us a lot of commands that He expects us to follow.

The Compelling Case for Personal Disciple Making

Over the last few years, I've been on quite a personal journey in ministry. For the majority of my 28 years in full-time ministry, I've invested my life in impacting China for Christ. This has included international student ministry, Chinese language learning, including a year participating in an intensive language study program in China, and for the last 10 years of this ministry season, serving the growth of the Church in China through rural Bible distribution and church building. I've enjoyed the whole journey and can earnestly say that it's been time well invested and has been a joy to be able to participate in God's work in these ways. In 2016, God began to change my focus as I learned about the 7400+ people groups around the world that are still unreached or unengaged through

---

29. Luke 6:46-48

several Bible distribution events that took us into more remote areas of rural China. As I looked at the Western Church to see what was being done to reach these dear people who are without Christ, I saw largely an apathetic Western Church, with little to no regard for reaching these lost souls. I felt a strong call toward solving the problem of bridging the gap between a Western church with so few Christians invested in Gospel sharing and disciple making, which leads to very few with a deep heart for the lost, both at home and abroad, and the 42% of the world's population that is still unreached with the Gospel. As I've been invested in solving this problem, one issue has come to the forefront that I've been investing quite a bit of my time, effort and energy trying to untangle.

I began to focus on the commands that we see Jesus giving to His followers, with an expectation that anyone who calls Him Lord and Savior would obey. Jesus' exhortation and my comments on Luke 6 from earlier apply to these commands, some 50 commands in all. You can find my full list of these commands in the resources section of this book, but these commands run the gamut from Jesus commanding us to Repent,[30] Love Your Enemies,[31] Do Unto Others,[32] and Love Your Neighbor.[33] As I was compiling the list, I realized a few things: First, it is an impressive list as we look at all the commands Jesus gives to His followers, and secondly, it would take some organization and intentionality to know the full list of commands Jesus gives and some discipline to be obeying them all. And it's clear that Jesus wants for us to obey them all. Case in point: In John 14, Jesus states that "whoever has my commandments and keeps them, he it is who loves me. And he who loves me will be loved by my Father, and I will love him and manifest myself to him."

To fully understand this passage in John 14, let me give you a quick

---

30. Matthew 4:17
31. Matthew 5:44
32. Matthew 7:12
33. Matthew 22:39

programmatic note about the word commands. In the New Testament, the Greek word can be translated in a couple of different ways. The Greek word ἐντολή, pronounced Entolē, can be translated into English either as commands or commandments, which make sense since the two English words are so close in meaning, and in fact, the word commandments is just a derived term of the word command. When we look at the dictionary definition of the word command, we see that it means to direct authoritatively, or to order.[34] In light of the 50 commands of Jesus, this passage in John 14 is pretty weighty, isn't it? Jesus Himself is saying, 'You say you love me, but in order to show me that you actually love me, do what I command you to do.' Yikes! To me, and I'm assuming to you too, that puts a whole lot of weight on knowing and doing the commands of Jesus, doesn't it? Because this is the type of passage where we can use my now famous formula[35] that the things we state we believe, our stated beliefs, plus our actual practice, that is whether we actually do the things we say we believe equals our actual beliefs. The application of my famous saying in this context is 'You say you love Jesus… How are you doing at obeying the commands of Jesus? This is how we can tell, and more importantly, how Jesus can tell if you love Him.'

In this line of thinking, as I was trying to figure out the problem God gave me to solve, I began narrowing down the list of commands of Jesus and focused on just two of the 50 commands that helped me find a solution I was seeking. In Mark 16, Mark is recording events after Jesus' resurrection and brief return to earth. The last words of Jesus that Mark records start off by Jesus saying, 'Go into all the world and proclaim the gospel to the whole creation.'[36] This command of Jesus has long been thought to be a direct command for His followers to be proclaiming the

---

34. https://www.merriam-webster.com/dictionary/command
35. It's not really that famous… I just say it all the time!
36. Mark 16;15

Gospel, both at home and around the world. We see it's a command of Jesus with the tell-tale imperative 'Go,' which is definitely authoritative. Interestingly, as the disciple Matthew records these same events after the resurrection, he records Jesus giving another command for us to "Go therefore and make disciples of all nations, baptizing them in the name of the Father and of the Son and of the Holy Spirit, teaching them to observe all that I have commanded you. And behold, I am with you always, to the end of the age."[37] This command is often thought to be the most popular of the passages associated with the Great Commission and depending on how you split up the commands found in this passage, it has either two or three commands in total. Clearly, we see the tell-tale imperative 'Go' again, meaning that Jesus is giving His marching orders for us all to be making disciples, and then separate commands to be baptizing these new disciples and teaching them the commands of Jesus in this passage.

So, let's take a deep breath and recap for just a moment. Jesus calls all of His disciples to be proclaiming the Gospel and making disciples. He then follows these commands up with 'it's when you do the things I command you to do, I know you really love me.' These passages and their overarching meaning bring me to a place of personal introspection to ask, 'How am I doing at knowing the commands of Jesus, and in particular, equipping myself with the tools to obey His commands to be proclaiming the Gospel and making disciples? I want to make sure I'm doing well in obedience because I certainly want to show Jesus how much I love him!' The apostles Peter and Paul drove those who received their letters to this introspection as well. Writing to the churches in Asia Minor, Peter wants to make sure that those in these churches, in their 'hearts honor Christ the Lord as holy, always being prepared to make a defense to anyone who asks

---

37. Matthew 28:19-20

you for a reason for the hope that is in you; yet do it with gentleness and respect.[38] Sharing the gospel requires a certain amount of preparation to know how to share and how to make a defense for the reason for the hope we have in Jesus. I recall the aforementioned 2 Timothy 2, as Paul is instructing the young Timothy, that "what you have heard from me in the presence of many witnesses entrust to faithful men, who will be able to teach others also."[39]

As I previously mentioned in the Introduction, there is an interesting phenomenon that happens as I share this message with Christians as I teach in Sunday School classes and preach on Sunday mornings. As I go through this biblical trail, of the commands of Jesus, and Jesus' instruction that it's when we do the things He commands we show Him we love Him, and that the implication then is that we should all be regularly proclaiming the Gospel and making disciples, the looks I get back from those listening is a bit surprising. As I share this message, the blank looks by most of those who are listening to me speak these words is really something to see. The message I get from their faces is, 'Mike, I have no idea how to do either of these things. You might as well be asking me to rebuild the transmission on your car.[40] A lot to be said here, about how church leadership should make sure that every person at their church knows how to share the Gospel and knows how to make disciples, but that's a topic for another book. We, as Christians, also have a personal responsibility that fall on us to know how to successfully share the Gospel and make disciples, and in regard to doing these two things, very few Western Christians today know how to do them. And that's the point of this book: I'm going to teach you through these pages all the steps necessary for you to begin helping another Christian grow in spiritual

---

38. 1 Peter 3:15
39. 2 Timothy 2:2
40. The modern automatic transmission has 500 to 300 parts and takes a skilled mechanic to rebuild!

formation through the development of a disciple making relationship. I promise that I'll try my best to leave no stone unturned and all the tools I have available, I will give to you and teach you how to use them.

Before I launch into this goal of mine, a couple of quick notes. First, I want to share with you a concern I've had that I touched on in the introduction as God put on my heart to write this book. As you are learning, at the core of disciple making is the idea that a spiritually mature Christian invests time with a person who has come to Christ, with the intent that person would invest in a third spiritual generation. Those of us that major in disciple making often talk about and work hard to have a reproducible ministry, since we want to see those we invest in investing in others. Because this is on the forefront of my mind and because you, as the reader, may have not ever had anyone disciple you, my big question with this book is: Can I create a disciple maker just by writing a book, helping you to be able to disciple others who will disciple a third spiritual generation? I asked several of my disciple making friends, and the consensus was that yes, it would be possible, if the reader took to heart all of the steps and instructions, and all of the disciple making tools given in this book. I mention this for a couple of reasons: First, I want you to know that I know that becoming a disciple maker by reading a book is not the normal way that this happens. Secondly, this is my way to implore you to make the most of whatever I'm able to give you in the way of steps, instructions and tools to help you become a disciple maker, thereby obeying the command of Jesus we find in Matthew 28.

Finally, I want to make sure you know that disciple making is not easy, and as you'll see through the pages of this book, there are a lot of 'ups and downs' as you go through the process of helping another Christian with their spiritual formation. You have wonderful successes and probably a few 'misses.' Please don't allow the 'misses' to discourage you too much and know that I firmly believe that there is as much benefit in the disciple making process to you as their will be for whomever you are helping in their spiritual formation. I've seen this happen time and time again, and the main reason this is true is clear: You have to be a fully devoted disciple of Jesus first before you can pour into the spiritual formation of another. I think the way God designed this process requires us to be also growing spiritually and growing in our understanding of the main truths of Scripture. As you'll see, the spiritual disciplines are a great tool in discipleship, and if you're not practicing some of them now, you'll want to be practicing them, not only for your own spiritual formation, but to be able to teach them to others.

Let's look next at us and our own spiritual formation. Let's go!

Chapter 2

Prepare Yourself to Make Disciples

One of my favorite things to do in my free time (I know, I'm a nerd!) is to get online and begin following what I call 'article trails.' Because of the nature of the internet, as I'm reading an article, I can quickly do an internet search about something new I'm learning about for the first time, and I can find a piece of information in that article to search and will read up on that new topic. This can lead to learning about all types of interesting topics, and at the end, I've learned about several new topics that I didn't know anything about! I love doing them, although I have to be careful because it can end up taking a lot of my time! Recently, as I was following one of these trails, I came across a legal principle called *Nemo dat quod non habet*, which is Latin for 'No one can give what they do not have.' In legal circles, it's often referred to as the Nemo Dat rule, which is the rule that states that a person who does not have adequate ownership of either goods or property cannot transfer the ownership of those goods or that property to someone else. Here's a simple example of the Nemo Dat Rule: Let's say that I have my bicycle stolen from me and the thief sells it to a man named Joe. As I'm investigating what happened to my bicycle, I find out about the theft and that the thief sold my bicycle to Joe. In addition to hoping the thief gets caught and faces justice for his crime, under this legal rule I'm able to go to Joe and demand that he gives me my bicycle back to me. Of course, Joe may say, 'But I just bought the bicycle from this guy, and I had no idea that it was stolen at the time that I bought it. I paid good money for this sweet bicycle!' Courts have held that *a true owner does not lose his or her title to goods simply because of the wrongful act of a thief who transfers possession of those goods to an innocent third party who acted in good faith in paying money to the thief'* for those goods.[1] While the rule seems unfair to buyers like Joe, it restores ownership to its rightful owner.

In the same way that you cannot sell what is not rightfully and legally yours, in discipleship you can't give to someone something you don't already have. This principle is an important one for me to cover before we get to the practical steps of disciple making because of the nature of disciple making. It's in the very nature of 2 Timothy 2:2 that we give to 'faithful men (people)' what we've been given and if you are not strong in your walk with Jesus and your understanding of Scripture, the discipleship process will not go as well as we would want it to. In this chapter, my hope is to flesh out what is the minimum spiritual formation that you need, sort of a 'lowest common denominator,' and still be equipped to make disciples that make disciples. Of course, I'd love to see all of us thriving in our walk with Jesus, but for the purposes here, let's have a look at where you would need to be spiritually. This look will be good for all of us because we can all use an examination of our walk and our faith from time to time. In fact, Paul speaks of this type of examination as he writes in 2 Corinthians, "examine yourselves, to see whether you are in the faith. Test yourselves. Or do you not realize this about yourselves, that Jesus Christ is in you?—unless indeed you fail to meet the test!"[2]

---

1. https://www.armstronglegal.com.au/commercial-law/the-nemo-dat-rule/
2. 2 Corinthians 13:5

In Order to Give to Others, Here's What You Need to Have Yourself

Accepted Christ as your Lord and Savior

I never get tired of hearing stories of how people come to first hear, then receive Jesus Christ as their Lord and Savior. It's actually a pretty amazing event to hear about, to have someone who is separated from God to hear about the free gift that God gives us through Christ. Peter's description of this event is one of my favorites as he writes, "that he might bring us to God, being put to death in the flesh but made alive in the spirit." Jesus desires that all come to Him, receiving Him into our lives. John writes about this amazing transformation in John 1, "but to all who did receive him, who believed in his name, he gave the right to become children of God."[4] As we truly receive Christ as our Lord and Savior, a number of things happen immediately in our lives: We become a new creation,[5] and are adopted into the family of God as God's child,[6] we are "sanctified" and washed clean,[7] given eternal life with God,[8] have God the Spirit living in us,[9] and our citizenship for all eternity gets a change in location![10] And this list is just a taste of all the wonderful changes that occur when we turn our lives over to Christ.

In order to effectively disciple another person toward spiritual formation, it is crucial that you have authentically and earnestly received Christ as your Lord and Savior, and that you are awestruck at what Christ has done in your life. Here's a quick test: Jesus gives another indication of how one may receive eternal life through Him in John 5:24, "Truly, truly, I say to you, whoever hears my word and believes him who sent me has eternal life. He does not come into judgment, but has passed from death to life." Does that fill you with thanksgiving and praise, knowing that you will

---

3. 1 Peter 3:18
4. John 1:12
5. 2 Corinthians 5:17
6. Galatians 4:5

7. 1 Corinthians 6:11
8. John 10:28
9. John 14:17
10. Ephesians 2:19, John 5:24

not be eternally separated from God through what Jesus has done for you
on the Cross? This authenticity is important as you prayerfully think about
discipling another person.

Growing as a Disciple of Jesus

In 2019, I wrote a book called, *What You Do Shows Who You Are:
The 6 Marks of a Disciple of Jesus* and it's been fun to see how God has used
it as people worldwide have asked the question, "OK, I've now 'received
and believed,' now what?" The book takes the reader through Six Marks
that one would see in their lives as a disciple of Jesus. Because each of the
Marks are pertinent here as well, let me briefly cover them, with the caveat
and encouragement that you might find that book helpful as you analyze
your potential effectiveness as a disciple maker.

1. A Disciple of Jesus has fully identified with Christ

The first mark of a disciple of Jesus is that they have identified with the
person of Jesus Christ—willing to openly admit that they belong to Christ.
At one point in His ministry, Jesus asked the disciples, "Who do you say
that I am?" Peter answered, "You are the Christ."[11] A disciple seizes on the
opportunity to identify himself with Jesus Christ. This Mark of a Disciple is
important for the disciple maker, since Jesus is the 'way, the truth and the
life'[12] and through an abiding relationship with Him comes life best lived.
As we read Paul's encouragement in Romans 1, "For I am not ashamed of
the gospel, for it is the power of God for salvation to everyone who
believes, to the Jew first and also to the Greek. For in it the righteousness of
God is revealed from faith for faith, as it is written, "The righteous shall live

11. Mark 8:29
12. John 14:6

by faith." The righteousness that the disciplee needs to be growing in is found in Jesus and the Gospel. As you'll see in later chapters, spiritual formation happens as we renounce everything else in our lives and as decisions, priorities or situations arise in our lives, we will deal with them in ways that draw us nearer to Christ, so that we gain more of and enjoy more of Christ. I could not see one being an effective disciple maker without a firm grasp on this mark.

2.   A Disciple of Jesus has a Supreme Love for Christ

Over the last 30 years that I've been a serious Bible student, I believe there is really no clearer theological principle in the Bible than God's desire for us to have a supreme, undying, incorruptible and incomparable love for Jesus, which is the second Mark of a Disciple of Jesus. We dive headlong into Matthew 22:36-40, into a passage commonly referred to as The Great Commandment. As the Pharisees were trying to trip up Jesus by asking a question they didn't think He could answer, since there are 619 Old Testament commandments, which the Sadducees and Pharisees couldn't seem to agree on which one was the greatest, Jesus makes His answer crystal clear:

"Teacher, which is the great commandment in the Law?" And he said to him, "You shall love the Lord your God with all your heart and with all your soul and with all your mind. This is the great and first commandment. And a second is like it: You shall love your neighbor as yourself. On these two commandments depend all the Law and the Prophets."

As it relates to becoming a disciple maker, loving Jesus deeply is so important since you'll be modeling for those you disciple what a deep love for Jesus looks like, and again, you can't give to someone else what you don't have. As you prepare yourself for disciple making, examine your own love for Christ.

3. A Disciple of Jesus is Obedient to the Bible

This may seem to be a silly addition to a list of what marks a disciple of Jesus would have, but in my work with One Eight Catalyst, I see unintentional (and maybe sometimes intentional!) disobedience to Scripture all the time. In fact, the very purpose for why One Eight Catalyst exists, which is the ministry I founded and now direct, rests on the reality that far too many Christians are not obedient to the Bible. Said another way, if Western Christians were excellent about Biblical Obedience, One Eight Catalyst would not need to exist! Simply put, a Mark of a Disciple of Jesus is that he or she is obedient to the Bible, knows God's Word, and seeks to obey the commands that are found in God's Word. Your obedience as a Disciple shows your heart for Jesus. Far too many in our churches today are good hearers of the word, but those who are true disciples in Jesus put that "hearing" into "doing." James, the brother of Jesus, makes this clear in his letter to Jewish Christians, "But be doers of the word, and not hearers only, deceiving yourselves."[13]

As a first step toward obedience to God's Word, a disciple of Jesus must have confidence in God's Word as an authoritative text that God has inspired and ordained. If the disciple wants to know God and hear from God, that communication happens primarily through the Bible. This

13. James 1:22

disciple knows that God saves by the Bible, He sanctifies by the Bible, and He comforts, edifies and does all spiritual work by the Bible. The foundation of all Christian endeavor is the Word of God.

4.   A Disciple of Jesus is Fruitful for Christ

Throughout the New Testament, a clear theological principle that Jesus and some of the apostles wanted to make clear: It is those who are abiding closely with Jesus that bear fruit in their lives for the glory of His kingdom. In addition to this, bearing good fruit is an important by-product of being a disciple of Jesus. Because there are 60 verses in the New Testament that mention the word 'fruit,' allow me to give a quick summary of what this looks like in the life of the disciple of Jesus. First, using a lot of agricultural references, we see that a good tree bears good fruit 'automatically.' Jesus states that "every healthy tree bears good fruit, but the diseased tree bears bad fruit. A healthy tree cannot bear bad fruit, nor can a diseased tree bear good fruit."[14] Jesus puts an exclamation on this point, stating that we see that good fruit is produced by the disciple of Jesus that remains close to Jesus, as Jesus Himself makes clear in John 15 as he says, "Whoever abides in me and I in him, he it is that bears much fruit, for apart from me you can do nothing."[15] Paul underscores this idea, that through the body of Christ, "so that you may belong to another, to him who has been raised from the dead, in order that we may bear fruit for God."[16]

There are consequences for those who have accepted Christ but are not bearing any fruit. Jesus doesn't mince words on this as He states in Matthew, "Every tree therefore that does not bear good fruit is cut down and thrown into the fire."[17] He reiterates the point in John 15, "Every

14. Matthew 7:17-18
15. John 15:5
16. Romans 7:4
17. Matthew 3:10

branch in me that does not bear fruit he takes away, and every branch that does bear fruit he prunes, that it may bear more fruit."[18] That brings out a few questions in my mind... First, how do we make sure we're bearing fruit? Jesus gives us a hint in Matthew 3, when he states that we must "Bear fruit in keeping with repentance."[9] We learned in the last paragraph that a lot of 'fruit bearing' happens as we abides in Christ and Christ in us. That is a good formula for fruit bearing! Secondly, what does good fruit look like? This is important, isn't it, given all of the wording about the importance of bearing fruit and what happens to us if we don't bear fruit. There seems to be a couple of layers to the answer to this question. For the disciple of Jesus that is abiding in Christ and planted in good soil, having received the promised Holy Spirit into our lives, Paul lays out nine 'fruits' we should be seeing increasingly in our lives. In Galatians 5 he writes, "But the fruit of the Spirit is love, joy, peace, patience, kindness, goodness, faithfulness, gentleness, self-control; against such things there is no law." It's a fun exercise to examine your life and see how you're doing in these nine areas, and if you find yourself lacking, taking extra time in prayer and through Christian accountability be working on your low spots. Additionally, as we learn to and are faithful in sharing the Gospel, we see fruit come from our efforts. Jesus states, "Do you not say, 'There are yet four months, then comes the harvest'?' Look, I tell you, lift up your eyes, and see that the fields are white for harvest. Already the one who reaps is receiving wages and gathering fruit for eternal life, so that sower and reaper may rejoice together."[20]

Finally, and in relation to evangelism and disciple making, we can always be praying and working toward those who we invest in to be also become 'fruit bearers.' As Paul was writing back to the church at Colossae,

18. John 15:2
19. Matthew 3:8
20. John 4:35-36

he was heartfelt in letting the Church know what he was praying for them as he prayed, "and so, from the day we heard, we have not ceased to pray for you, asking that you may be filled with the knowledge of his will in all spiritual wisdom and understanding, so as to walk in a manner worthy of the Lord, fully pleasing to him: bearing fruit in every good work and increasing in the knowledge of God."[21]

5. Filled with Love for Others

A primary distinguishing characteristic of a disciple of Jesus should be a deep and committed love for their brothers and sisters in Christ. In the surveys and studies I've seen over the last few years on the top reasons non-Christians don't want to attend our churches is that they see how we in the Church treat each other and want no part of it. Not only is the committed disciple preoccupied with his Lord's glory, but he also is filled with God's love. A distinguishing mark of being a follower of Christ is a deep, sincere love for brothers and sisters in Christ. Perhaps this distinguishing mark of the committed Christian is the most significant of all in terms of practical living because we tend to be around people all the time! And we see that the Bible has plenty to say on the topic. Go through this sampling of passages on the topic:

From Jesus: *"A new commandment I give to you, that you love one another: just as I have loved you, you also are to love one another. By this all people will know that you are my disciples, if you have love for one another."*[22]

---

21. Colossians 1:9-10
22. John 13:34

From 1 John: Whoever says he is in the light and hates his brother is still in darkness. Whoever loves his brother abides in the light, and in him there is no cause for stumbling.[23]

For this is the message that you have heard from the beginning, that we should love one another.[24]

We know that we have passed out of death into life, because we love the brothers. Whoever does not love abides in death. Everyone who hates his brother is a murderer, and you know that no murderer has eternal life abiding in him.[25]

And this is his commandment, that we believe in the name of his Son Jesus Christ and love one another, just as he has commanded us. Whoever keeps his commandments abides in God, and God in him. And by this we know that he abides in us, by the Spirit whom he has given us.[26]

Beloved, let us love one another, for love is from God, and whoever loves has been born of God and knows God. Anyone who does not love does not know God, because God is love.[27]

If anyone says, "I love God," and hates his brother, he is a liar; for he who does not love his brother whom he has seen cannot love God whom he has not seen. And this commandment we have from him: whoever loves God must also love his brother.[28]

---

23. 1 John 2:9-10
24. 1 John 3:11
25. 1 John 3:14-15
26. 1 John 3:23-24
27. 1 John 4:7-8
28. 1 John 4:20-21

In my way of thinking, whenever Jesus commands us to do something, we should perk up and do it! And clearly this 'new commandment' stuck with John. In fact, none of the other three gospel books in the New Testament record Jesus saying this 'new commandment.' Could it have been that John, named as the disciple that Jesus loved, heard and took note of this commandment when the others did not? We will never know in this life, but clearly John was deeply impressed by the command for Christians to have a deep love for other Christians. John emphasizes a few aspects of this love in the passages of 1 John: First, Jesus commanded us to love each other and states that whoever keeps the commands of Jesus has God living in him. Also, I am struck by how many times John says, 'If you hate your brother, you do not know God and you are a liar.' Why did John choose to call this person a liar? Simply put, if you say you love Jesus and hate your brother or sister, you are only saying you love God. Your stated belief does not match your actual behavior.

6.   Deny Yourself Daily

As the disciple of Jesus receives a call to follow Him, he is clearly called to deny Himself and take up his cross daily, as we see Jesus stating in Luke 9, "If anyone would come after me, let him deny himself and take up his cross daily and follow me. For whoever would save his life will lose it, but whoever loses his life for my sake will save it. For what does it profit a man if he gains the whole world and loses or forfeits himself? For whoever is ashamed of me and of my words, of him will the Son of Man be ashamed when he comes in his glory and the glory of the Father and of the holy angels."[29] In the study of this passage, I've often asked myself and others,

---

29. Luke 9:23-26

'How do we know if we are "'taking up our cross daily and following Jesus well"' as disciples of Jesus?' Over the years, I've found these questions to be a helpful exercise, taken from the website www.gotquestions.org:

- Are you willing to follow Jesus if it means losing some of your closest friends?
- Are you willing to follow Jesus if it means alienation from your family?
- Are you willing to follow Jesus if it means the loss of your reputation?
- Are you willing to follow Jesus if it means losing your job?
- Are you willing to follow Jesus if it means losing your life?

Following Jesus doesn't necessarily mean all these things will happen to you, but are you *willing* to take up your cross? If there comes a point in your life where you are faced with a choice—Jesus or the comforts of this life—which will you choose?[30] This Mark of a Disciple is the most challenging for many Christians because to fulfill this mark in your life, you must choose whom you are going to live for. There is much to lose from an earthly perspective in order to completely follow Jesus! When confronted with this choice, the decision you make demonstrates who Jesus is to you and the place in your life that He holds.

Spiritual Disciplines

As we think about preparing ourselves to become a disciple maker, there's one final topic I'd like to write about here, and it's the topic of Spiritual Disciplines. Despite their essential nature in the life of a disciple of Jesus, I'm afraid that they are not talked about enough in our churches today. Just like our daily lives require discipline for us to function correctly,

---

30. "What did Jesus mean when He said, "Take up your cross and follow Me"?" Accessed October 15, 2018. https://www.gotquestions.org/take-up-your-cross.html

there are spiritual disciplines that help us in our walk with Jesus. Simply put, the spiritual disciplines are practices found in Scripture that promote spiritual growth and formation among believers in the gospel of Jesus Christ. They are habits of experiential Christianity and devotion, that have been practiced by God's people since biblical times. These spiritual disciplines are primarily used to aid and guide our growth toward maturity and therefore are to be executed in our lives on a regular basis. These spiritual disciplines are important not only for your own walk, but as you see later in this book, as you will begin meeting with someone weekly in a disciple making relationship, and they will become an essential tool for you to use.

Over the years as I've talked with Christians about the Spiritual disciplines, it seems like many believers don't see the benefit of adding certain disciplines to their Christian life. For them, it may seem to be discipline without direction. But in a number of places in the New Testament, it's clear that we should strive to become more holy as Christ is holy. In Hebrews 12 for example, we're called to "Strive for peace with everyone, and for the holiness without which no one will see the Lord."[31] Without this holiness, that is to say, without Christlikeness or godliness, we will not see the Lord, regardless of how much you've attended church or participated in Christian activities. And while I must state boldly that it's not our pursuit of holiness that qualifies us to see the Lord, as we accept Christ as our Lord and Savior, we are given the Holy Spirit.[32] The presence of the Holy Spirit in our lives then causes new 'holy desires' we didn't have before we received the Holy Spirit. We now hunger after time in God's word we didn't have before. Before we received the Holy Spirit, we had no desire to share the Gospel through evangelism or to spend time

31. Hebrews 12:14
32. Ephesians 1:13-14

memorizing God's word through Scripture memory. It is this hunger created by the Holy Spirit that compels us to strive 'for the holiness without which no one will see the Lord.' And so, we "discipline ourselves for the purpose of godliness,"[33] knowing that the Holy Spirit makes godliness our purpose, and so we add discipline into our lives to achieve this purpose. In his wonderful book on the Spiritual Disciplines, Donald S. Whitney states "I will maintain that the only road to Christian maturity and godliness passes through the practice of Spiritual Disciplines. I will emphasize that godliness is the goal of the Disciplines, and when we remember this, the Spiritual Disciplines become a delight instead of drudgery."[34] Because the goal of discipline making is to pass to others what you have learned, implementing the Spiritual Disciplines in your life is so important as a prerequisite for what you'll be learning in the pages ahead.

Over the years, I've developed a list of 10 spiritual disciples that I consider essential toward spiritual formation, and you'll be seeing these spiritual disciples sprinkled throughout the book. Toward the back of this book, there is a Resources Section that will have certain resources for you to use as you begin your first discipleship relationship. One of those resources is a list of 24 topics that you will want to work through with your new disciplee as you begin meeting weekly. A second resource in this section is a descriptive listing of each of the 10 spiritual disciplines, including what they are and an example or two of where you'd practice them. For now, here's a list of these spiritual disciplines as a primer. I'd also encourage you to go through the list in the resources section and begin implementing those that you're not already implementing into your daily walk with Christ. This truly is a 'you can't give to someone something you

---

33. 1 Timothy 4:7
34. Donald S. Whitney, Spiritual Disciplines for the Christian Life (NavPress, Colorado Springs)

don't already have' situation and before you begin in a disciple making relationship, it's a good idea to be practicing these in your own life as well.

- **Bible Reading**
- **Prayer**
- **Scripture Memory**
- **Worship**
- **Evangelism**
- **Fasting**
- **Journaling**
- **Serving**
- **Stewardship**
- **Silence and Solitude**
- **Perseverance in the Disciplines**

As you can see, while I want to make this book a resource for all Christians, the 'lowest common denominator' of the disciple maker is still a pretty high bar. But this bar is set at a level where God wants us all to be: pursuing and loving God with all our heart, soul, mind and strength. It is this pursuit in a person, fully aware of our struggle against flesh and blood, that makes one prepared to make disciples that make disciples.

Let's go!

Chapter 3

Intentionality in Disciple Making

Intentionality. It's not a word we hear very much in our Christian circles, but I think it's a crucial piece of both being and making disciples of Jesus. Let me explain.

The word Intentionality means to do something with intention, which means what one intends to do or bring about.[1] To have an intent to do something is to have something in mind as a purpose or goal, to have a plan. Here's a quick example: My wife and I have three adult children, and when we started having children, we both had the intention to raise our children in a household that trusted God in all things and we wanted to always be pointing them toward Biblical truths for their lives. Joshua 24:15 was a key passage for my wife Sherie and I, "But as for me and my house, we will serve the LORD." Our purpose was to raise children that would someday trust Christ as their Lord and Savior and live all their days surrendered to Christ. Having this purpose in raising children, we had to be very intentional about how we would go about accomplishing our intent, which included making many decisions about what our lives would look like, how would we spend our time, what activities would we as a family participate in and what entertainment we would watch, just to name a few. In the process of making these decisions and parenting with this type of intentionality, there were outside forces that told us and told our

---

1. https://www.merriam-webster.com/dictionary/intention

kids that we didn't need to have this type of seriousness, but we did not waver, and we did our absolute best to parent our children in a Christ-like manner. Did we make mistakes? Yes, no parent is going to parent children perfectly, but we sure wanted to try to do the best we could.

As I've studied the Bible over the years, I think there is an intentionality that God calls us to in our relationship to Christ as well. Always my first example here is the apostle Paul's admonition in Philippians Chapter 1. If you haven't spent time in Philippians lately, may I highly recommend that you spend some time reading Paul's letter to the church at Philippi. His letter to this Roman colony overflows with joy and thanksgiving, and we see Paul's heart for evangelism and for His Lord and Savior. We see the intentionality of Paul's life starting in verse 21 as he writes, "For to me to live is Christ, and to die is gain. If I am to live in the flesh, that means fruitful labor for me. Yet which I shall choose I cannot tell. I am hard pressed between the two. My desire is to depart and be with Christ, for that is far better. But to remain in the flesh is more necessary on your account. Convinced of this, I know that I will remain and continue with you all, for your progress and joy in the faith, so that in me you may have ample cause to glory in Christ Jesus, because of my coming to you again."[2] In the life of Paul, for as long as he was alive, he wanted to live for Christ! There is intentionality pouring through this passage of Philippians, to live every day for Christ. In addition, even though he'd love to have departed to be with Christ, it was his intention to use every day that God gave him to be used by Christ to bear fruit for Christ. He also had the intention to be a blessing to the church at Philippi to help their progress in their faith and to be sure their joy and reason to praise Christ is in Christ alone.

2. Philippians 1:21-26

The question then has to be asked: Do we live our lives with that type of intentionality toward doing everything we can, putting all our time and resources toward living for Christ and allowing that intentionality to direct our lives? Our lives in Christ should give our lives on earth a deep intentionality to not only live for Him, but to obey the commands He's given us to proclaim the Gospel and make disciples. Paul understood this idea. In verse 22, he writes, "If I am to live in the flesh, that means fruitful labor for me." Stop for just a minute and think of what it would have to take for you to orient your life to truly believe that for every day Jesus gives you, it'll just mean you have more people to share the Gospel with and more Christians, new and old, to help grow in their spiritual formation (i.e. 'fruitful labor'). This is important because as we saw in earlier chapters, these activities are a primary calling for all of us.

In my work now with One Eight Catalyst, one of the biggest challenges I have in my ministry is to help people see that many times their actions don't match up with their values as a believer in Jesus. In many of our lives, there is an intention-action gap, sometimes called the value-action gap, which occurs when what we say we value, things like 'Jesus is my Lord and Savior' and 'I love Him' and 'The Bible is the inspired Word of God,' doesn't match our actual actions or beliefs about those statements. In doing some reading about the value-action gap, it is a gap commonly found amongst all of us in one form or another. For example, many of us see this play out in our lives as we make resolutions every January to get into shape, only to not exercise and get in shape. Instead, we spend that time on the couch watching the next episode of our favorite television show that we find easier and more gratifying at the moment. In our relationship with Jesus, we can see the same gap in areas like having the intent to read through the Bible in a year and finally learning how to share the Gospel. I wish I could be with you now and give you this direct encouragement about your life in Christ: If you have accepted Jesus as your Lord and Savior, you will show Him how much you love Him if you regularly are sharing your testimony and the Gospel with others around you. And if you never share the Gospel and continue to have no clue how to make a disciple, I assume by using the value-action gap stated above, you really don't love Jesus very much and need to re-embrace what Christ has done for you on the cross, falling in love with Jesus again. I'm sorry to be so blunt, but I'd be happy for you to prove me wrong.

One of the things that I can assume about you if you're reading this book is that you do love Jesus, and even if you're not doing a very good job of showing Him your love for Him through your actions, you want to make changes in these areas. If that's you today, I say 'Yay!' and that I'm all in to help you become someone who both knows the commands of Jesus and has an intentionality around obeying those commands as well. Because that's all its going to take! If you're like most Christians I know, you don't know how to share the Gospel in obedience of Mark 16:15 and you don't know how to make a disciple in obedience to Matthew 28. All it would take, however, for your actions to match your intentions is for you to say, "I don't know how to do either of those things, but Jesus is commanding me to do them, so I'm going to figure out how to do them if it's the last thing that I do!" Remember that living with intentionality just means that we make a goal and have a purpose in mind, and as it comes to our lives that we're living, living with an intentional goal in mind is a wonderful way to live.

As a first step, I often recommend to people that they develop a mission statement for their lives, which is not something that many people think about since they believe mission statements are only for companies or organizations. But if we are going to live lives intentionally for Christ, knowing what the purpose for our lives would give us a goal to shoot for. As an example, let me take verses I've already used here to create a 'starter' mission statement for each of our lives.

I live every day for Christ,[3] loving Him with everything I am and everything I have.[4] I desire my days to be filled with fruitful labor[5] as I seek to proclaim the Gospel[6] and make disciples[7] with my life.

Your actual life mission statement may and probably will look a bit different, but you can begin to see that if you determined to live your life with this as your life's goal, things would begin to change about how you lived, how you spent your time, energy and resources. A great place to start is in prayer, just begin asking God what your mission statement should be and begin being attentive to what He says to you. I'll be praying that God gives you a wonderfully unique and meaningful mission as a start of a life now lived with intentionality. With the direct commands we see from Jesus, the instruction through the rest of the Bible and the intense need for Christians to be about proclaiming the Gospel and making disciples, I believe it is impossible for us to claim to be Christ's called out ones and live without intentionality. And even more striking is that we'll never impact the world for Christ and be a part of God's redemptive work in the world without knowing God's purpose and plan for our lives and the intentionality to see that plan through to the end. It is those Christians who live unintentionally who see the spiritual lostness of those without

---

3. Philippians 1:21   6. Mark 16:15
4. Matthew 22:37   7. Matthew 28:18-20
5. Philippians 1:22

Christ and do nothing to enter into how God wants to use them. It was John C. Maxwell, author and speaker who wrote, "An unintentional life accepts everything and does nothing. An intentional life embraces only the things that will add to the mission of significance."[8]

Living our lives with the intention to see fruitful labor from the proclamation of the Gospel and the making of disciples begins by doing two things. The first, which I mentioned above, is to recognize you may not know how to do these things, but because it is now part of your life's purpose, you're determined to learn how to do them. The second action here is for you to have a determination to get the training you need to live out your mission statement, which may include training on how to share the Gospel and make disciples. As it relates to learning how to share the Gospel, there are a lot of online tools and YouTube videos that can help. I would recommend however that if your home church is not regularly teaching the congregation how to share the Gospel, go to your pastor and say something to him like this: *"Pastor, I know that Jesus is commanding me to regularly share the Gospel, but I don't know how. Will you teach me?"* This may lead to training classes, and it certainly signals to church leadership that they have people at their church who want this type of training. And it is my intention to give you the training necessary to know how to start a disciple making relationship in the pages and chapters that follow.

The Tools of the Disciple Maker

The first step in the training necessary for you to begin making disciples is to learn about the tools of the disciple maker and why tools are important for the disciple maker. As we all know, tools play an important role in doing any job with intentionality. It'd be hard for the bricklayer, for

8. John C. Maxwell, Intentional Living: Choosing a Life That Matters (Center Street 2015)

example, to do a proper job without his brick and pointing trowel, brick hammer, levels and bolster and cold chisels. Each tool has a specific purpose and without one of them, the job of expert brick laying would be incomplete. In disciple making, there are also tools that enable the disciple maker to train up those they are discipling.

As we talk about the tools of the disciple maker, I reiterate my definition of disciple making as *the process by which a Christian* **with a life worth reproducing** *commits himself for an extended period of time to a few individuals who have trusted Christ, the purpose being to aid and guide their growth to maturity and equip them to* **reproduce themselves in a third spiritual generation.** Because we want to be disciple makers that are intentional, our purpose is to aid and guide a few individuals' growth and maturity, equipping them to reproduce themselves in others, and there are tools that will help us become these types of disciple makers.

What is a Disciple Maker's Tool?

Tools that are used by disciple makers can take on a number of different forms, although we'll be using two primary types of tools in this book: Either in the form of a worksheet that you can use as you begin discipling another Christian, or in the form of a method that is helpful for spiritual formation. For example, Scripture memory is a Spiritual Discipline and a wonderful tool for spiritual growth and includes both types of tools found in this book. There is both a worksheet that teaches you how to begin memorizing Scripture and each of the 24 weekly topics have two memory verses for each week.

Examining what is a disciple maker's tool includes a description of what it is not. The first thing that it is not is a common mistake many church leaders make. Disciple making cannot be a program at your church, using a book or curriculum that you buy and try to use for disciple making. Since much of disciple making is life-on-life and requires a large investment by the one discipling into the life of the one being discipled, exclusively going through a book or curriculum is not sufficient for disciple makers. Tony Miltenberger, co-host of The Practitioner's Podcast, mentioned on a recent episode that by using only books and/or curriculum in disciple making, we're subject to the author's interpretation, which may or may not line up with Scripture.[9] In a broader sense, we want to veer away from a programmatic approach to using tools in disciple making. As you begin meeting one-on-one with another Christian in disciple making, you'll want to address the issues that are keeping the disciplee from growing and use tools in a way that meets their individual needs.

Why Are Disciple Making Tools Important?

Disciple Making tools are important for several reasons. The first reason is that both Jesus and the apostle Paul used tools in their ministry, and we want to be making disciples in the same way that Jesus made disciples. The primary tool that both of them used was the Word of God. As Jesus was praying to God, he proclaimed, "I have given them your word… Sanctify them in the truth; your word is truth."[10] Jesus' intent was that as He had used the Word of God in his earthly ministry, those who He invested in would be set apart for a sacred purpose. And throughout the New Testament, as Paul was traveling on His evangelistic and church planting journeys, he would do much of His ministry in the Jewish synagogues when he would arrive in a new town, reasoning with them using the Scriptures. Acts 17 gives us one such example. "They came to

9. Justin Gravitt and Tony Miltenberger, The Practitioner's Podcast, Season 1, Episode 12
10. John 17:14,17

Thessalonica, where there was a synagogue of the Jews. And Paul went in, as was his custom, and on three Sabbath days he reasoned with them from the Scriptures, explaining and proving that it was necessary for the Christ to suffer and to rise from the dead, and saying, "This Jesus, whom I proclaim to you, is the Christ."[11] Paul also gives us a good reason why all of our tools should be Biblically based in 2 Timothy 3, "All Scripture is breathed out by God and profitable for teaching, for reproof, for correction, and for training in righteousness, that the man of God may be complete, equipped for every good work." And we certainly want all people who we are discipling to be complete in Christ and equipped for every good work!

Disciple Making tools are also important because good disciple making tools will help you and those that you are discipling grow in the spiritual formation process toward becoming a disciple that makes disciples. As you begin discipling others, disciple making tools should become an extension of yourself as a way to help others grow spiritually. This works primarily as you are using in your own walk with Christ the same tools that you are using in disciple making. The tools you'll find here will be just as useful in the hands of those that you are discipling as they are in your hands. I'll give you tools that are very reproducible, so that as they see their effectiveness in their own growth, they will have confidence that they can use them as they reproduce in others. Tools are also important because a good disciple making tool can help everyone with various learning styles to learn the content. A good tool can be understood by everyone who desires to grow in their walk with Jesus.

As we start in the next chapter with the next step in the disciple making process of praying about and beginning to select the people you'll

---

11. Acts 17:1-3

start meeting with in a disciple making relationship, all the key tools you'll need to use and that I'll be referring to you'll find in the resources section of this book. Each tool has a description of what it is, how it's used and the Scriptural background for that tool. As you begin meeting with someone one-on-one, each tool is also available for download and printing to be used as a handout at www.EquippingDepot.org/tools.

Here we go!

Chapter 4

Finding Faithful People

Being a small business owner is hard and the process of starting a new business is difficult enough that some people, even if they have a good idea for a business, won't dare to 'take the leap' and start their own business. Starting a business lacks a lot of the glitz that you see from the entrepreneurs that end up becoming successful, and in fact, many of those who ended up making it 'big' started out working from their basement or garage. For every Elon Musk or Bill Gates, there are hundreds of thousands of entrepreneurs who can't get their business to sustainability. The latest statistics tell the true tale. According to data from the Bureau of Labor Statistics, approximately 20 percent of small businesses fail within the first year. By the end of the second year, 30 percent of businesses will have failed. By the end of the fifth year, about half will have failed. And by the end of a decade, only 30 percent of businesses will remain — a 70 percent failure rate.[1] Being a small business start-up means that you're most likely going to be scraping by for some time, you'll doubt your abilities because things usually don't go as you'd planned for them to go and you'll most likely have those closest to you question or doubt whether you're doing the right thing.

Of all the issues that the new entrepreneur will face, many experts say that the recruitment and selection of good employees is the most

---

1. https://www.fundera.com/blog/what-percentage-of-small-businesses-fail

crucial element of running a successful organization or company. A good selection process, including the writing of a job description for the open position to receiving and interviewing potential candidates is key in finding talented and competent employees. The end result of the selection process, the hope is that those hiring can match the right people with the best blend of skills and experience to succeed, both professionally and personally in the new role. But because it costs the company time and financial resources to onboard new employees, if a wrong decision is made, it can cost the company a lot and can be a real source of frustration and consternation.

Selection in the Disciple Making Process

The first step in the process for anyone who wants to obey Jesus' command to 'Go and Make Disciples' is to begin praying about and thinking through who they should select to begin a disciple making relationship. And just like the selection process for the small business owner wanting to expand their business to acquire new employees, the selection process in disciple making is one that must be done with care, and if not, can lead to frustration and consternation of the one doing the selecting. Let's look now at what this selection process can and should look like. The selection of people you'll be investing in is important first and foremost because not every Christian is ready to be discipled at the time you'll want to ask them to enter into a discipleship relationship. Jesus gives us a fantastic explanation of this in Matthew 13 in His parable of the sower, sometimes referred to as the parable of the Four Soils.[2] This is one of the few parables of Jesus where Jesus He teaches the parable, then explains the meaning of the parable shortly thereafter. In this parable, we see a sower

---

2. Matthew 13:1-9, 18-23

who is scattering seed, and as Jesus tells us in His explanation, this 'seed' is the 'word of the Kingdom,' better known as the Gospel. As people are hearing and responding to the Gospel, the sower's seed lands on four different types of ground. Some of the seed lands on hard ground along a path and does not take root, becoming bird seed, which Jesus tells us that represent people who hear the Gospel, but it never takes root in their lives. Some of the seed landed on rocky ground without a lot of soil, and the seed starts to grow but doesn't have enough good soil to grow deep roots and withers in the sun. Jesus explains that this is someone who hears the Gospel and receives it well at first, but at the first sign of persecution or trouble, they fall away from this new faith. Still other seed lands in with the thorn bushes and as the plants begin to grow, the thorns choke out the plants that begin to grow. Jesus explains that these are people who after hearing the Gospel, their new faith gets choked out by the cares of this world and the desire for wealth. And finally, we have the seed that lands on good soil that is very favorable toward producing "grain, some a hundredfold, some sixty, some thirty."[3] Jesus tells us that it is this final grouping of people that you'll be looking for to talk to about starting a disciple making relationship with. So how to you find people who are 'planted' in good soil, thereby ready to grow spiritually? I have 4 categories for you to look for as you begin thinking about meeting one-on-one in a disciple making relationship.

Jesus Invested in Ordinary Men

In our churches, there always seems to be that person who seemingly has all aspects of their life and family 'all together.' They seem to have the wealth, the right career, the great hair, and a great family. People

---

3. Matthew 13:8

like being around them and it seems like life has given them all the perks.
As you begin to consider discipling another Christian, you may think that
this would be the type of person you'd want to invest in first. We obviously
don't want to overlook these types of people, but as we look at the types of
people that Jesus invested His time in, He selected ordinary men who were
not at the top of the social class at the time. And although we only know
the professions of six of the twelve disciples, these certainly were working
class type people. We know that five of the disciples were fisherman or
were around the fishing industry. Matthew, of course, was a tax-collector,
and was not universally admired in his day. It's also interesting to note that
the 12 disciples that Jesus selected were also had distinct personalities,
flaws and all. These were not cookie cutter personalities... they were their
own people. Peter, for example, was one who did not hold back from
speaking his mind and was a bit impetuous. James and John, called by
Jesus 'the sons of thunder,'[4] were serious about their faith and even more
serious about protecting the ministry of Jesus.[5] And then there was
Thomas, famously dubbed 'Doubting Thomas,' because of his 'I have to see
Jesus with my own eyes' attitude on the news the other disciples had seen
Jesus after His crucifixion. Don't be afraid to select someone who doesn't
fit traditional molds. The men that Jesus selected as His disciples were
overlooked by the religious class at the time. In fact, we get a wonderful
glimpse into where these disciples were in their society as we read about
the exploits of Peter and John in Acts 3 and 4. After healing the lame
beggar in Acts 3, Peter and John preach in Solomon's portico, which leads
to their arrest and subsequent trial before the elders, rulers and scribes. As
they listen to Peter talk in his own defense, one of my favorite verses stands
as an inside look into the lives of these disciples. "Now when they saw the

4. Mark 3:17
5. Luke 9:54

boldness of Peter and John, and perceived that they were uneducated, common men, they were astonished. And they recognized that they had been with Jesus."[6] The religious leaders of the day noticed a couple of things about these men, first that they had been with Jesus. The leaders could tell the seed had been planted in good soil. And secondly, that they were uneducated and common men.

As you begin thinking and praying about who to begin selecting, remember not to overlook those who seem uneducated and common. It's not uncommon that the people who you would first think about would be the flashy, popular people, but if we take heed of Jesus' example, many times those who are not 'first on people's list' are those who actually become the best disciples and wonderful disciple makers.

Jesus Prayed Before Selection

Occasionally, I'll hear a teaching or sermon about how Jesus chose to impact the world for the Kingdom of God through His selection process. In this sermon, one of the main points usually is that Jesus did not choose to impact the world for the Kingdom of God through preaching to massive crowds or through great grandstanding efforts on his behalf. While He did preach to some crowds, His modus operandi was to invest the bulk of His time with 12 men, knowing that an intense amount of His time with these twelve men would be the best way for Him to impact the world for the Kingdom of God. In hearing these sermons, I'm always struck by the power of the idea of how Jesus decided to impact the world. Think about it for a minute: Since He only had 12 slots to fill, I'm sure He wanted to have really good selections. As we begin considering who we should select, let's remember that before Jesus made His selections

---

6. Acts 4:13

He prayed about it. He took the concern about who to select to God and allowed God to determine who these 12 men should be. "In these days he went out to the mountain to pray, and all night he continued in prayer to God. And when day came, he called his disciples and chose from them twelve."[7] While it's not a requirement to pray all night as Jesus did, we certainly want to take the decision to God in prayer, asking Him to reveal to us who to select as we consider who to invest time in. In my own life, it's often been a week or more in prayer, as I may have two or three people that have risen on my radar, and before I begin the process of asking them to consider meeting together, I certainly want to be taking those names to God in prayer.

There's a couple of reasons why praying about who to select is so important. First, of course, we want to have confidence that the people we are selecting are people that are actually God's selections. I'm sure Jesus had His pick of whoever He would have liked to select and having the confidence that His picks were God's picks allowed Jesus to select with confidence. We want to have this same type of confidence. Secondly, as you'll see in future chapters, you're inevitably going to run into bumpy roads on your disciple making journey. Knowing that you're on the bumpy roads with someone who God told you to select to invest your time into will give you an assurance to power through the bumpy times.

We're looking for people who are FAT

As you pray about who to begin investing time in, we're looking for FAT people. And while the percentage of overweight and obese people increases throughout the world, this is not the type of fat I'm referring to here. FAT is a longstanding acronym in the disciple making world that

---

7. Luke 6:12-13a

stands for Faithful, Available, and Teachable. It's a great acronym to help you remember the type of person you're looking for to begin a disciple making relationship.

Faithful

People who are faithful are steadfast and dependable. They are able to commit to something and stick with it. Jesus addresses this as He states, "But let your 'Yes' be 'Yes,' and your 'No,' 'No.' For whatever is more than these is from the evil one."[8] When a faithful person says Yes to something, you can count on them doing it. Jesus puts a high value on people being faithful as a condition toward them being trusted in life and ministry. "One who is faithful in a very little is also faithful in much, and one who is dishonest in a very little is also dishonest in much. If then you have not been faithful in the unrighteous wealth, who will entrust to you the true riches? And if you have not been faithful in that which is another's, who will give you that which is your own?"[9] Paul instructed Timothy to invest his time in "faithful men who will be able to teach others also."[10] We're looking for people who demonstrate a desire to be faithful to God and to you and your new relationship together. You'll be looking for someone who will faithfully show up to your appointed time together, ready to learn and receive instruction.

So how can you tell if someone is faithful? First, observe their spiritual life and see if they are faithful in their walk with Jesus. You'll be able to tell in some simple conversation if they are spending time with Christ and in God's Word. How are they in other areas in which they've committed like church attendance, faithfulness in their relationships and with their friends? These areas are discoverable simply by unleashing the

8. Matthew 5:37 NKJV
9. Luke 16:10-12
10. 2 Timothy 2:2

power of observation. What do you see in their lives and how do people closest to them react around them? How are they at managing finances? You'll be able to pick up on clues in these areas of their lives. This is an important attribute because while the unfaithful Christian may have a desire to grow as you begin walking with them in discipleship, they won't follow through on the appointments and assignments you'll give them in your times together. They will say all the right things but will not follow through on completing them.

Available

A quick study of the life and times of the Old Testament prophet Isaiah gives us a good starting point on availability. At the start of his prophetic ministry, God gave Isaiah both a message and a vision to deliver to the nation of Judah and a vision. After confronting his own unworthiness, Isaiah states in Isaiah 6, "And I heard the voice of the Lord saying, '"Whom shall I send, and who will go for us?'" Then I said, "Here I am! Send me."[11] Isaiah made himself available for whatever and however God may want to use him. And in a culture where the primary obstacle to meeting in a disciple making relationship is people being too busy, observing their availability both to God and to others is of primary importance. Obviously, you'll want to begin meeting with someone in discipleship that remains available to meet with you and available to other people as they begin meeting with them too. This availability will keep the discipling relationship they've started with you as a priority. I've often thought that hidden within this characteristic is a full belief and understanding that God brings certain people and circumstances into our lives and as well as being available to run and roll with whatever God

11. Isaiah 6:8

brings our way. This is important because it's this understanding of God's greater plan and a belief that God can use my life however He wants despite my imperfections that has led to some of the greatest moments of my life.

Discern a person's availability by his willingness and availability to meet with and invest in others. Does this person designate time to listen, study, and learn from others? Are they accessible when called upon? Do they have a regular quiet time with God, consisting of reading the Word and praying? Availability is measured by a willingness to serve God and be available for whatever may come their way. This is important because people whose 'plate is always full' will not make a good person to disciple. I've started meeting with several men who told me they were interested, but as it came time to meet together, they clearly could not make it a priority. Since we all only have a certain amount of time every day and every week, we want to be investing in people who want to return that investment with a time investment of their own. As I often say, 'People will invest time into the things that are most important to them.'

Teachable

Teachability is quite important as you're looking for who to begin investing in toward a disciple making relationship. It would be hard to enter into a disciple making relationship with someone who wasn't teachable. A teachable Christian is one who has a desire to learn and apply what they are taught from God's word. They take what they learn from God's word and can apply toward greater godliness in their lives. They are also open to rebuke and correction in areas of sin in their lives. King David understood the importance of correction as he writes, "let a righteous man strike me—it is a kindness; let him rebuke me—it is oil for my head; let my head not refuse it."[12] Because ultimately you're looking for people who, under your guidance, will apply God's word to their lives toward godliness. You have to know that it's really hard for God to work in a heart that does not easily and readily receive instruction (a hard-soiled or rocky-soiled heart). Through all the reading I've ever done in this area and in my long personal experience, this characteristic is a real deal breaker. The person you select must have a teachable spirit. Full stop. They have to be open to Biblical instruction as well as your guidance and counsel as you both are meeting together. A person that you may be interested in selecting may have all types of crazy talent and abilities, but if they are not teachable, you cannot have a successful disciple making relationship that leads to a 2 Timothy 2:2 outcome.

In this area of being teachable, I have some personal experience that may be helpful. In my upbringing, my parents were not ones to show much affection toward me, and my dad was particularly cold toward me. In addition, my dad was one of those people who always had to be right and never was able to take advice from others. As the combination of those things affected my early years, it made me a pretty cold-hearted know-it-all once I got to my 20's. After I received Christ as my Savior as a senior in high school, I'm sure the first man to disciple me a couple of years later I'm sure spent a lot of time praying for me! In fact, he easily could have (and maybe should have)[13] passed by me as one who was not ready for discipleship since I was the prototypical unteachable Christian in those days. I was interested in consuming and understanding Scripture, but I wasn't ready to apply much of God's truth and allowing Scripture to transform my life. I was way more interested in head knowledge and not as

---

12. Psalm 141:5
13. Although I'm so glad he didn't pass by me!

available for heart change. My story illustrates a couple of points: I can tell you from experience that you're going to have a hard time with someone who is not teachable, and it may be that you'll have to not meet with them because they're just not ready in the teachability area. On the other hand, if God is telling you to hang in there with them and continue meeting, just know it may be a couple of years before God does enough work in their lives for them to go from head to heart.

You've Identified a FAT person… Now What?

Let's say you've identified someone that you'd like to ask as a good candidate to begin meeting together regularly toward spiritual formation… Yay! But how do you ask them to begin meeting together? No worries! Before I end this chapter, let me walk you through the process. This is important because asking someone to begin meeting together in a discipleship relationship can be awkward and you may have some anxiety toward 'the ask.' But don't worry, not only will I help you with the ask, but it gets easier each time you ask, it is just those first couple of times that may be hard for you.

Preparing for The Ask

As you think about what you want to say to them as you prepare to ask them, I'd encourage you to think along these lines:

Why do you feel they would be a good candidate?
What have you seen in their lives that make you think they would be a good candidate?
What has God done specifically in your life to lead you to ask them?

Think through the answers to these questions and take your analysis of their place on the F.A.T. scale, combined with what God has told you in prayer. If you have peace in all these areas, it's time to move to the ask stage!

Why Giving them a Formal Invitation is Important

It's important that you ask them directly if they would like to begin meeting together on a regular basis toward spiritual formation for several reasons. In the same way that the Bible tells us that to be a follower and disciple of Jesus, we must count what it costs to follow Jesus. Giving future people you meet with the chance to count the cost of going deeper into an authentic life-on-life relationship with you is crucial. Jesus explicitly tells us that "If anyone comes to me and does not hate his own father and mother and wife and children and brothers and sisters, yes, and even his own life, he cannot be my disciple. Whoever does not bear his own cross and come after me cannot be my disciple. For which of you, desiring to build a tower, does not first sit down and count the cost, whether he has enough to complete it?"[14] Because this person is entering into a relationship that will be hard at times, stretching them toward greater Christlikeness, it's a good idea to allow them to count whatever costs may be associated with this new relationship. And 'counting costs' always involves recognizing and agreeing to some terms first, which I'll help you think through in the next section. But giving them the chance to know what they are getting themselves into and to think and pray through this is healthy.

Formally asking them if they would enter into this relationship also allows them to take ownership in the process as they are willingly entering into this new relationship. It also allows them, as they say Yes to your ask,

---

14. Luke 14:26-28

to get 'all in' and commit fully to whatever God may have in store.

It's Asking Time!

Once you've thought through the answers to the questions above, it's time to ask them to enter into this new relationship. Depending on where you are're at around the world, you may have different traditions around where people meet together to fellowship with one another. But this will be something like asking them initially for a meal or a hot or cold beverage. This initial ask could be something like this:

Hey, (their name here), over the last few years, God has given me a heart for spiritual growth, and I'd love to get have some time over coffee to talk about that and I'd like to ask you to participate as well. What time/day works well for you?

Of course, you're going to make this fit the way you talk, but it is just a simple invite to talk about spiritual things over a meal or a beverage. It's nice to keep it somewhat lighthearted, with the idea that you'd love to connect with them and have a chat.

Once you meet together with them, the real ask is a bit more involved. Here are the key things you'll want to cover as you talk to them and ask them to enter into this relationship together:

- Since you probably already have some type of relationship with them, share with them about discipleship and that you've been praying about who God would want you to disciple.
- You can share a bit about the command Jesus gives to 'Go make disciples' in Matthew 28 and that you want to be obedient in the areas

Jesus has given commands.

- Explain the vision behind 2 Timothy 2:2 and that you want to be one who is entrusting to reliable people the things you've learned, with a heart toward those people entrusting those same things to others.

- Explain that you believe God has brought the two of you together for a reason.

- Then comes the ask: 'Would you pray about meeting together weekly and developing a deeper relationship toward spiritual growth?'

At this point, they will probably have some questions. In either your answers to those questions, or following those questions, be sure to emphasize that you're hopeful they will take this new relationship seriously, that a discipleship relationship is a two-way venture where they will be able to hold you accountable in areas where you're weak and that you'll be probing deeper and deeper into character issues and developing life and ministry skills. And as I mentioned earlier, in the resources section of this book, I have your first 24 weekly lessons for you all to go through. Remember, the goal in discipleship is for both parties to grow more like Christ, to fall even deeper in love with Christ and for the two of you to pass along the growth and the topics learned to a third spiritual generation.

As you prepare to ask people to join you on this journey, may I make a quick recommendation: Take all I've given you here and make some notes on a separate sheet of paper. Organize your 'ask' on paper first, then begin practicing it until it becomes comfortable for you to say from memory. This will help you ask confidently, hitting all the points you'd like to make. And remember, I'm praying for you as you begin asking people to join you in this new journey!

Final Thoughts

As I end this chapter, a couple of final thoughts: First, I hope you've seen in this chapter that not everyone is ready to be discipled at the time you may be ready to ask them. They may be faithful and teachable, but too busy and not available. They may be available and teachable, but not faithful. This is where we can trust God with these people and begin the process of praying for them. Just because they are not ready doesn't mean they are not good people or that they don't love Jesus. In their journey with Jesus, they just aren't there. And just because they are not ready to be discipled, doesn't mean they won't be in the future. You may see real growth in their lives and in two or three years, they may be ready, and you may be available to disciple them.

Secondly, there's a bit of discussion and disagreement in the disciple makers world about whether it's possible to disciple a non-believer. Having gotten this far in this book, I think you know what side I come down on this, but suffice it to say that I do not believe that it is possible to disciple a non-believer. I broach this topic mainly because you may be tempted to skip steps when it comes to evangelism, thinking that jumping right to discipleship would be more expeditious. Our main issue here simply drives to the definition I gave you earlier in this book on what discipleship is, 'Discipling others is the process by which a Christian with a life worth reproducing commits himself for an extended period of time to a few individuals who have trusted Christ, the purpose being to aid and guide their growth to maturity and equip them to reproduce themselves in a third spiritual generation.' It's this 'a few individuals who have trusted Christ' part that I'm concerned about here. Someone who is not a 'believer and receiver' of Christ has not yet trusted Christ and that has several implications when it comes to discipleship. A person who has not trusted Christ does not have the Holy Spirit in their lives, which means they do not have that guide helping them become more like Christ. Also, a non-believer is not concerned about becoming more like Jesus and has no interest in being aided and guided in growth to maturity in Christ. Instead of trying to disciple a non-believer, spend time with them, guiding them to a genuine faith in Christ through the process of evangelism. There are plenty of tools you can use to share Christ, including the Bridge Illustration or the Three Circles Illustration, my two favorites.

Now that you're ready to ask someone to begin a discipleship relationship, in the next chapter, I'll take you even deeper into what these regularly scheduled times look like, including a deep dive into a 'behind the scenes' look at the philosophy and mind set you should have as you begin meeting with someone one-on-one. We'll look specifically at how your time should be scheduled during these meetings and how you know whether the people you disciple are growing spiritually. I'm excited for you as you trust God for big things as you continue this journey.

Let's go!

Chapter 5

Fruitful Disciple Making Meetings

It's no secret that we need friendships. They are one of the most important relationships that we have as people. Friends fill the gaps in our lives with laughter and offer support to us in times of need. The best friendships are ones where both people are intentional about their shared commitment to the other person's growth and well-being. These types of friendships are not friendships of convenience or friendships that are built simply on similar interests. They also take a bit of effort on both sides to nurture and maintain the friendship. This intentionality spreads to include a commitment that no matter how different your schedules may be or how far away you live from each other, you make time for each other.

As you've selected someone to begin a discipleship relationship, you'll find that while there are some similarities between a friendship and this discipleship relationship, there are also differences in that the goals are a bit different. Before we walk through what this one-on-one meeting looks like, allow me to touch a bit on a scale that disciple makers use to distinguish between how much you should focus on being relational verses the intentionality that is required in this disciple making relationship.

Intentional vs. Relational on the Disciple Makers Scale

I'm glad to have the space in this chapter to write to you about this scale in the disciple making relationship because there are important concepts for you to consider as you begin meeting with someone one-on-one. Understanding and preparing to handle the Intentional vs. Relational scale sets you up for better success. Here's how this works: When you begin meeting with someone in this new relationship, you'll want to be both relational, meaning that you'll want to get to know them personally and take interest in their personal lives, and you'll want to enter into this relationship with intentionality. This intentionality is important because your goal will be to not only see them grow in their spiritual formation, but you also want them to eventually be able to take what they learn from you and disciple other people in the same way.[1] As is the case with all of us, we all enter into new relationships stronger in either being more relational or more intentional, so it's important to know at the outset in which one you are stronger. This helps you know a couple of things. First, we all like to work within our strengths and second, we'll know which side we'll need to work harder to improve in.

So how do you know which side you're stronger in? For the person who is stronger on the relational side, this is a person who can talk to people and make friends easily. They can make connections easier with people and naturally begin asking questions with people about things that are important to that person. Topics like family, work, and shared life experiences come up in conversation, and generally speaking, people like to be around other people who are good relationally, since we all like talking about ourselves! In a discipleship relationship, if you're good relationally, you'll want to use this skill to make people feel comfortable

---

1. 2 Timothy 2:2

around you. The challenge here is that there does need to be intentionality, that is, you need to have a goal and a plan as to why you're meeting together. For people who are stronger at intentionality, these are people who tend to be more goal-oriented, list making people. These people have a plan for everything and are good at coming to a meeting with someone with an end goal in mind and are focused on reaching or completing specific tasks to achieve a planned outcome. This idea that the purpose of a new discipleship relationship is to see that person grow in their walk with Jesus and to be able to see them then disciple other people is not hard for these types of people. But as you can see, while it's good to have intentionality in this new relationship, it would be easy to drive the new disciplee away as they feel they are just a task to accomplish, and the disciple maker is not interested in them personally. Finding a balance here is important as you begin discipling others.

As we find balance in this scale, Jesus gives us a good example of how to do both of these well. Jesus was definitely relational with the 12 disciples and others who were closest to Him during His earthly ministry. He considered these 12 men as friends. "Greater love has no one than this, that someone lay down his life for his friends," Jesus told them this before doing that very thing. He continues in John 15, "You are my friends if you do what I command you. No longer do I call you servants, for the servant does not know what his master is doing; but I have called you friends, for all that I have heard from my Father I have made known to you."[2] As we begin discipling others, we want them to know that we care for them and have their best interests in mind, as Jesus did with His 12 friends. The Gospel accounts of the life and times of Jesus show us that He really did like being around these people in that He spent a lot of time with them. We

2. John 15:13-15

see Jesus walking around from city to city with the disciples. We see Him eating together with them, both separately and with other people. We see Him washing their feet, in a sign of humility. I can only imagine what all that time spent with the disciples did to their understanding of what the mission was Jesus came to accomplish. This reminds me of what I've often said about why I like United States governmental officials engaging with leaders of hostile and/or reclusive countries for high-level meetings of various types. For the cameras, we always see the high-level meetings of the top leaders, many times around a table or seated close to one another, shaking hands. But it's always the lower-level government employees and the meetings and relationships that they are having that gets me excited. During these meetings, the lower-level government employees learn about how the United States works and they can take that understanding back to their country to help make changes. In the same way, you'll want to be relational with those you are discipling, because they will know you care for them and have their best interest in mind, and they will learn from you in ways that you may never know.

Jesus was also quite intentional in His time with the 12 disciples as well. His intentionality came from a keen sense of what God had sent Him to do and how He wanted to do it. We see this mission clearly: He wanted all people to love God with everything they had,[4] to proclaim the good news that saves all men from an eternity without God[5] and to make disciples of all nations,[6] not wanting any people from any people group to go without this Good News.[7] To accomplish this mission, He spent intentional time with them, then sent out the 12 two-by-two to preach, to heal and to have authority over unclean spirits.[8] We also see a direct intentionality when Jesus is calling the disciples to follow Him:, "Follow

---

3. As they old saying goes, 'More is caught than taught.'   6. Matthew 28:18-20
4. Matthew 22:37-38   7. Matthew 24:14
5. Mark 16:15   8. Mark 6:7-12

me, and I will make you fishers of men."[9] Amongst these men who dropped everything to follow Jesus, there was a clear goal in mind: I want you to be with me so we together can fish for men, so none will be eternally lost.

How do we translate all of this as we begin making disciples? I have a few thoughts that may be helpful: First, as you begin meeting with people in a discipleship relationship, you'll want to have a plan going into the first meeting. This plan, hopefully, will have its basis around to help them grow in Christ, and enabling them to make disciples eventually themselves eventually. It was the early American intellectual Benjamin Franklin who said that "If you fail to plan, you are planning to fail!" And for each meeting, you'll want to come in with a plan for that particular meeting together, with specific goals to accomplish. Setting the example of having a goal in mind going into a meeting is a good example to set. As English author Lewis Carroll said, "If you don't know where you're going, every road will take you there." But as you'll see later in this chapter as I discuss the specifics of what these meetings looks like, you want to invest time in the new relationship and get time with them, even outside of your regularly scheduled meetings. My colleague and Navigator staff member Justin Gravitt has a great illustration here. In a recent episode of his podcast, he mentions that finding the right balance between relational and intentional is like taking a shower. If we're all intentional, delivering content, focusing exclusively on our agenda for the meeting and not tuning into how they are doing personally, it's like taking an ice-cold shower. We can get clean, but everyone will want to jump right out. The opposite can be true as well if we focus exclusively on the relational side, which is like having a hot shower that keeps getting hotter. It may be nice at first, but it can get too hot, and you won't accomplish the goal of the shower, which is

---

9. Matthew 4:19

to get clean.[10]

I love this illustration because it does a good job of showing that we need both relational and intentional components in this new relationship. And this is especially important because we want them to see that there is a difference between this discipleship relationship and a friendship. While you may also be friends, this relationship has a different objective and hopeful outcome.

Starting the One-on-One Meetings

After you've gone through the selection process, it's time to begin meeting with your people in a one-on-one setting. These meetings are generally weekly, although I've had a couple of men I've discipled who, because of work or family commitments, were available twice a month, which still worked out well. As you schedule the meetings together, finding a suitable time and place is important. As I've met with men in discipleship, I've divided the time into three different categories. Because I like to ask for between 60 to 90 minutes for each session, this gives me the opportunity to divide the time into thirds between Investment in the Relationship, Teaching on Ministry and Life Skills, and Character Development. Let me go through each of these three to help you know how to delve into each of the three categories.

Investment in the Relationship

"And he appointed twelve (whom he also named apostles) so that **they might be with him** and he might send them out to preach and have authority to cast out demons."[11] I love this passage from Mark 3, because we see how Jesus started in His relationships with the 12 disciples: He went

---

10. https://www.justingravitt.com/practitionerspodcast-transcripts/s1ep14
11. Mark 3:14-15

through a selection process, then wanted these men to be with Him. In the same way, you'll want to both spend time with your disciplees outside of the meeting, doing things together and in the meeting, asking about their lives, checking in with what is going on with their family. As former United States President Theodore Roosevelt often said, "People don't care how much you know until they know how much you care." Two key thoughts here: First, over time as you meet with this new person, be sure to schedule time outside of your regular meetings to watch sports together or have them over for dinner. These types of times together help them know you really do care about them. Secondly, in the meeting time, you can use some of the time to get an update on their lives, showing genuine interest in them, their families, and their career. If your meeting time was 90 minutes, 20 to 25 minutes could be spent on this relationship building time. The word of caution here is that while this time is important, the danger is that you don't want this light chatting about them and their lives to take up all the time either. Watch that you get on to the other two sections as well, since those are the real 'meat' of the one-on-one meetings.

Teaching on Ministry and Life Skills

In this section of your regularly scheduled meetings, this is where you'll initially go through the 24 topics I've included in my weekly topics that you'll find in the back of this book. I'm including these topics as a way for you to have content to go through with your new disciplee. These weekly topics fit here because this portion of your meetings are where you're teaching them ministry and life skills that lead to a stronger relationship with Jesus and the tools to enable them to find victory over the enemy in Christ. With my weekly topics, I've worked hard to give you what

I've found to be the best topics to accomplish these goals. You'll see that each of the topics has 6 sections and as you prepare for each meeting, just make sure you've read through each of the 6 sections and can talk intelligently about each of them. As you see with each weekly topic, I'm helping you define each particular topic, the reason that this topic is important, Scripture verses that speak about the topic, some practical application of what you should have learned in going through the topic and any other helpful resources about the topic that help you teach them. I've also given you two Scripture memory verses that you all can be memorizing together that refer to each topic.

As an example of how this time could be spent, let's take the first topic on my weekly list: Assurance of Salvation. As you meet and talk about this topic, you'll want to make sure that the person you're meeting with knows they have been saved from an eternity without Christ and that they know the Scripture verses that give them this assurance. As you talk through this topic, you can see in the weekly topic entry for this topic, it will give you the opportunity to share the Gospel again with this person if they cannot adequately describe for you their own salvation. As you go through each section for the weekly topic, make sure they know questions can be asked, and as you go through the Scripture verses that are included, feel free to add your own Scripture verses that you may find in your preparation for your meeting. Finally, I'll have practical ways to apply what you all have learned as you study Assurance of Salvation. One of the benefits of having a list like I'm providing here of topics to discuss is that it'll give you the opportunity to refer back to them as you go along in your discipleship relationship together. If the person you're meeting with shows any 'regression' on any topic, you can go back and refer to what you've already learned and refresh their minds around the discussion you all have already had. For a 90-minute meeting, I would dedicate 40 minutes to this section of a meeting together.

Character Development

This final section of a typical one-on-one meeting, this is probably the hardest for most people since it's not a regular part of how we've built relationships with others in the past. This is the section of your time together where as you will see problems in their character that are hindering their ability to be more like Christ, and you'll want to dedicate time talking about that flaw. Let me give you an example: Let's say that as I'm meeting with someone regularly, I begin to see that they seem to have a problem with anger. Obviously, someone who has a problem with anger has a blind spot as to what is going on in their lives and how it is affecting both their walk with Christ and potentially, their relationships with others. We know enough from Scripture that God doesn't want us to live in anger, therefore in this part of their lives, they are not in line with either Scripture or God's best for their lives. From King David's instruction in Psalm 37 for us to "refrain from anger, and forsake wrath! Fret not yourself; it tends only to evil,"[12] to Paul's directive in Ephesians 4 for us to "let all bitterness and wrath and anger and clamor and slander be put away from you, along with all malice. Be kind to one another, tenderhearted, forgiving one another, as God in Christ forgave you,"[13] we know God does not want us to live our lives in anger. As you prepare for this meeting where you've decided that God is asking you to talk to them about their anger, pray through how exactly God may want you to address this with them. Have a few Scripture verses ready to share with them about what God's way would be in this

---

12. Psalm 37:8
13. Ephesians 4:31-32

area and go into the meeting confident that God will give you the words to say. As you prepare to talk to them about this blind spot, remember the goal here is for them to become more like Christ. It shouldn't be done with an 'I'm better than you' attitude, but in a loving way that indicates you are talking about this because you want their best. As you develop this relationship, let them know they have the freedom to bring up character development topics to you as well.

If this section of your time together is done well, it can be of great benefit, both to their walk with Christ and to your relationship together. I know that in my own life, the most rapid growth in my walk with Christ occurred as people brought up these issues. I believe this happens because they are blind spots I couldn't see, below my awareness level. And while I recognize that it must have been hard for them to say something about these issues to me, I'm sure glad they did. I hope you'll find both the courage to say something, and that you find that it actually strengthens your relationship with your disciplee. I've heard a number of people over the years say that if you really care for someone and you want to see God's best for their lives, it's not loving and caring to allow the sin or serious issue you see in their lives to go unaddressed. And as it relates to our 2 Timothy 2:2 goal, you want them to make disciples that are also aware of sin issues, which we all have. Creating a model for them that we don't allow these issues to go unresolved is a goal we should all have in meeting with people in discipleship. Finally, addressing character or sin issues in the lives of those you're meeting with allows you to revisit those issues from time to time, seeing that they are finding victory and celebrating that victory with them!

Handling the Disruptions

In discipleship meetings, there will occasionally be issues that come up that will need to be addressed. For example, what happens if the person you're discipling says that they have a vacation coming up or a work event that will prevent them from meeting at your regularly scheduled time? When these disruptions come up, my motto has been 'be patient yet tough.' Obviously, we all know that issues come up in our own lives and in the lives of others. Something happens at our kids' school, and we get a phone call to come in, or the boss asks last minute for us to come in an hour early. As you remember in from Chapter 4, we're looking for people to disciple who are faithful people. In addition, if you've laid out the commitment that a disciple making relationship requires, these types of interruptions normally work themselves out. As an example, your disciplee tells you that they have a two-week vacation coming up and will have to miss the next two meeting times. You should take them at their word, and tell them that you would appreciate it if they continued working on the Scripture memory verses they've been working on, and to contact you if any personal prayer issues come up while they are gone. If this is a faithful person, they will only miss the session that they told you they would miss, and you'll be able to re-engage that third week. What happens then if every other week, there are multiple interruptions to the meeting schedule, and they miss more meeting times than they make? This is where 'patient yet tough' comes into play and may be an indication they are not ready for the commitment that you laid out before you started meeting together. As you'll read in Chapter 7, some people aren't quite ready to be discipled, and because your time is limited, it may be better to wait until they have the commitment and enthusiasm to meet together in this way.

Discipleship Growth Process: What does growth look like?

Before I end this chapter, let's look at what growth looks like in the discipleship process. This is important because it would be good for you to know how you're doing in your discipleship and what fruit your effort is bearing. There's a lot of material about this, some of which seems to me to be very academic, so allow me to bring this to the most simplistic level so we can all understand what we should be looking for in the life of our disciplees. As you continue meeting with your disciplee, in addition to my six marks of a disciples mentioned in Chapter 2 that you can use to gauge spiritual growth, here is a list of 5 attributes of a growing disciple in Christ.

Transformed Mind

I appeal to you therefore, brothers, by the mercies of God, to present your bodies as a living sacrifice, holy and acceptable to God, which is your spiritual worship. Do not be conformed to this world, but be transformed by the renewal of your mind, that by testing you may discern what is the will of God, what is good and acceptable and perfect. - Romans 12:1-2

This exhortation from Paul in Romans 12 is a great starting point when it comes to what we should be looking for in those who we disciple. As they are meeting with you weekly, they are exposed to God's word, which works on their hearts and reveals areas of sin that lead to repentance, and they will conform less to the world and more to the heart and will of Christ, leading to becoming a living sacrifice for Christ. This leads to a transformation of the mind, which is the key to the Christian life.

Technically, the Greek word translated as repentance is *metanoia*, which actually means 'a change of mind.' As we disciple men and women and they are convicted of their sin through time in God's word and in the accountability that a disciple making relationship provides, we're praying to see a conviction in their hearts that translates into action. Our prayer for them is the same prayer Jesus prayed for those He invested in:, "Sanctify them in the truth; your word is truth."[14]

Changes in Behavior

> Therefore, if anyone is in Christ, he is a new creation. The old has passed away; behold, the new has come. -2 Corinthians 5:17

A renewing of our mind leads then to changes in behavior, no longer being conformed to the world. A person who has received Christ and is allowing the Holy Spirit to work in their lives through the admonition of God's Word and godly people in our lives. We literally become new creatures! In our western context, it's easy for us to grow complacent in our life in Christ, forgetting whom we really serve and what our God is completely capable of doing. From the drug addict to the guy addicted to porn, to the lady fighting an eating disorder, the God who is able to do 'abundantly more than all we could ever ask or imagine'[15] wants to set us free and give us a new life in Christ! As we disciple men and women, we'll be looking for changes in their actions, attitudes, and behaviors. Those that were controlled by anger are now exhibiting the love, joy, peace, and patience found in the indwelling of the Holy Spirit. People who had no patience for certain people now have a love for others like

14. John 17:17
15. Ephesians 3:20

never before. Be looking for these changes as you disciple people as a marker that God is using you in mighty ways!

Fully Obedient to the Bible

For the word of God is living and active, sharper than any two-edged sword, piercing to the division of soul and of spirit, of joints and of marrow, and discerning the thoughts and intentions of the heart. - Hebrews 4:12

Although I've already written at length about this topic, both as a mark of a disciple of Jesus and in the 'if the Bible says it, we want to be people who do it,' we'll see in the growing disciple of Jesus an increased interest in spending time in God's Wword, both through reading and study and the memorization of the Bible. This attraction to God's Wword leads to a 'right or wrong' discerning of their thoughts and intentions and you'll be able to tell that God's is at work in their lives in this way.

Growing Heart for the Lost

Do you not say, 'There are yet four months, then comes the harvest'? Look, I tell you, lift up your eyes, and see that the fields are white for harvest. Already the one who reaps is receiving wages and gathering fruit for eternal life, so that sower and reaper may rejoice together. - John 4:35-36

Anyone who is growing spiritually will begin to realize that there are a lot of other people, both in their local area and around the world who do not yet know Jesus. As I have already written in previous chapters, I truly do not believe that someone who has received Christ into their lives can also have no heart for the lost or interest in sharing the Gospel with those who have not yet heard or received it. In the growing disciple, you'll see an interest in proclaiming the Gospel and making disciples. And you can fuel that fire towards the lost as well, both through the several topics in my weekly topic list, and through setting an example for them as one who is already sharing the Gospel. These stories of what God has done in your life can be quite inspirational to the new disciple who is gaining a heart for the lost.

Increasingly used by God to advance His Kingdom

And this gospel of the kingdom will be proclaimed throughout the whole world as a testimony to all nations, and then the end will come.
-Matthew 24:14

I have heard of many amazing stories about what God has done in the lives of people who are fully surrendered to Christ in the area of advancing God's Kingdom around the world. We, as Christians, are God's Pplan A for reaching the world for Christ and He doesn't have a Plan B. In those you disciple, you should be able to have increasingly more challenging conversations about how they sense God may be nudging them in this area. As I already mentioned, Mark 16:15 and Matthew 28:18-20 stand out to me because they are direct commands from Jesus, so it seems to make sense that the growing Christian would be increasingly aware and concerned about how God may want to use them in the proclamation of the Gospel and the making of disciples. And because I'm misunderstood about this topic sometimes, let me clarify one thing. While not everyone is called to proclaim the Gospel overseas, every disciple of Jesus is called to proclaim the Gospel. For some, that may be in their neighborhoods. One doesn't need to go far, maybe just one house over, to find people who need to hear the Gospel. Also, even for those called to only reach their neighborhood or their city, we are all also called to see that the Gospel is proclaimed throughout the world. For some, this may look like, 'Yes, I'm active in sharing the Gospel in my local area AND through my church. We cooperate with and support those called to go internationally to proclaim the Gospel.' For the growing disciple in Christ, you'll see their 'antennas' go up as they learn about how God may want to use them to advance God's Kingdom.

I'll be praying for you as you begin meeting with people one-on-one, and I'm thankful you have the commitment to obey the command Jesus has given you to 'Go and Make Disciples.' In the next chapter, I'll walk through with you through some of the greatest obstacles in disciple making, together with tips and tricks for you to find victory over the obstacles toward disciple making success.

Let's go!

Chapter 6

Obstacles You'll Face in Disciple Making (and what to do about them!)

It seems like, in life, there are situations where we have all the information we need to accomplish a task and still find it hard to get the task done. If you've been an adult for any amount of time, I think you know what I mean. This reality hits me particularly when it comes to carpentry. Over the years, I've built shelves around my house, and every time I try to get them just right, I can't quite do it. It's weird for me because I know how to draw out what I'm looking to build, measure and mark the wood, make the precise cuts, and glue the pieces together, but inevitably, it rarely turns out the way I'd hope it would. This is not to say that I haven't built some things that have turned out OK, but I clearly don't have the eye that others have in this area. What makes this even more frustrating is that I don't know how to do carpentry any better! For many of us, parenting is in the same category. I remember my wife and I reading all the books we could get our hands on before having kids and going into parenting thinking we had that subject mastered! Of course, as kids came along, we found out quickly that there were things about parenting that we couldn't learn from books alone.

Over the last five chapters, I've given you all the information you'll need for you to begin obeying the command of Jesus to begin start making disciples, and yet, as you get started in the disciple making journey, you may feel, at first, like I do with carpentry. If you've read the chapters and gone through the resources section of this book, if I've done my job as the author of this book, you now have the basic information you need. As you start making disciples, you'll find that there are some obstacles along the way that may keep you from being as successful as you're hoping to be. In this chapter, allow me to walk you through some of the obstacles that you'll inevitably find along the way with some solutions to those obstacles to help you power through.

Apathetic Busyness

Let's face it: We're all pretty busy. Especially for those of us in North America, we generally perceive the busy person as high status and the more we believe that one has the opportunity for success based on hard work, the more we tend to think that people who skip leisure and work all the time are of higher standing. This perception leads us to intentionally have a lot going on, between work, kids and grandkids' sporting events, school, friends, and family, and this leaves us with little time for anything else. And this busyness pervades our churches as well. As the saying goes, "Idle hands are the devil's workshop,"[1] right? When we add church activities to all the other busy body activities, it's easy for the modern Christian to think, 'Who has time for the disciple making process?' Combining this busyness with an overall apathy toward obedience of the commands Jesus has given us leads to an obstacle you'll find in making disciples, both in yourself and in those you hope to disciple. This apathy may come from one of many different sources, the most important of which would be unrepentant sin in the life of the believer. What makes sin so harmful is that it drives a divide between us and God. When we don't deal directly

---

1. Proverbs 16:27 TLB

with sin, we can become so entangled that it becomes easy to ignore the voice of God and the direct commands of Christ. The result of this entanglement is that when our Lord and Savior, Jesus Christ, calls us to make disciples, our response becomes, "No thank you. I'm not interested, and I have too much else going on in my life." As Spence Shelton, lead pastor at Mercy Church of Charlotte, North Carolina states in a recent blog post, "When we willfully disobey Christ's command to make disciples *and don't feel convicted about it,* we're in a dangerous spot. If we treat the commands of Christ like *suggestions,* we are acting in our own power. We're being deceived and ruled by sin."[2] Paul illustrates for us well in Ephesians 1 who Christ is to the disciple of Jesus as he writes, "And he put all things under his feet and gave him as head over all things to the church, which is his body, the fullness of him who fills all in all." We pursue Christ, knowing Him with our whole hearts, and knowing when He gives marching orders, we obey them because we love Him with our whole hearts.

The first step toward attacking this obstacle is in our own lives, we confess to God areas we have been most rebellious. Secondly, we commit to obeying every command Jesus gives us to the best of our ability. Committing to be available to make disciples in any way God would see fit requires a re-evaluation of our time and availability. As we ask others to join us in this disciple making journey, they will see we have already 'counted the cost' of becoming a disciple maker and we can speak from experience of our own commitment when we ask them to do the same. As I stated earlier in this book, we will make time for the things that are most important to us, and any command from Christ automatically becomes important to the disciple of Jesus.

---

2. https://jdgreear.com/two-obstacles-keeping-us-from-making-disciples/

Combating busyness and apathy in others as you invite them into a disciple making relationship is a tricky situation. As I've been thinking about this conundrum, I have remembered a phrase I learned early on in my disciple making journey. The phrase, 'Many Aspire, Few Attain' came from the title of a sermon preached in 1975 by Navigator staff member Walt Henrichsen. If you've never heard this sermon, may I highly recommend it to you.[3] While the sermon is more about people who were pursuing Christ deeply in their younger years, but as they got older, their fire for Christ waned, I think we could use the title in our context as well. As you begin asking people to join you in disciple making, you'll find many who aspire to grow in their walk with Jesus, but many will not have the fire to follow through. I mentioned in Chapter 4 how important it is to find men and women who are Faithful, Available and Teachable. These are the ones who not only will aspire to grow in their walk with fancy talk and good intentions, but they will follow through and will pursue what you have to teach them through your times together in God's Word. This selection process is how you fight through busyness and apathy in those you desire to disciple. Simply proceed with those willing to meet together and set aside any aspirations to meet with those who are not Faithful, Available and Teachable, trusting that in time, God may change their hearts from one who only aspires only into one who will truly want to attain.

Our Own Fear and Lack of Trust in God

As I've coached and counseled others toward having a disciple making ministry, fear, and a lack of trust in God, has to be one of the greatest obstacles. Because we generally don't fear tedious and unimportant

3. https://soundcloud.com/brministries/many-aspire-few-attain-walt-henrichsen

tasks, the fact that we may have some level of fear as we begin a disciple making ministry indicates the significance and importance of making disciples. This fear, manifested many times as 'I don't have what it takes to make disciples,' or 'I'm going to make a fool of myself if I even try,' really indicates a lack of understanding about what Christ has already done in our lives and God's providence and power to use us in any way He would see fit. In our minds, the rationale many times goes something like this:. 'If I ask person A to begin meeting with me in discipleship, what if they say no? What if I start and I'm no good at it? What if I fail at this, and they tell others how bad I am at disciple making?'

Encouragement from Matthew 28

If this is you today, let me encourage you from God's Wword as we remember that Jesus Himself is the one commanding us to 'Go and Make Disciples.' A review of Matthew 28 would be helpful here:
And Jesus came and said to them, "All authority in heaven and on earth has been given to me. Go therefore and make disciples of all nations, baptizing them in the name of the Father and of the Son and of the Holy Spirit, teaching them to observe all that I have commanded you. And behold, I am with you always, to the end of the age."[4]

Let's take a slow and deep dive into this passage. I think there are four parts of this passage that we need to remember and remind ourselves of often.

---

4. Matthew 28:18-20

1. All authority in heaven and on earth has been given to me

If the one commanding us to make disciples has been given all authority in heaven and on earth, I think we may be able to trust Him to use us in disciple making as He would want to use us. Earlier in Matthew 11, Jesus tells us that "All things have been handed over to me by my Father..."[5] All authority. All things. All given to Jesus, who now says to each of us, 'You go and make disciples.' As the one with all authority over all things, I think He's got you covered when He gives you a heart for disciple making and the people to disciple. We don't have to worry about the outcome because He's got our back. One of my all-time favorite passages about our own fear is in Isaiah 41, "fear not, for I am with you; be not dismayed, for I am your God; I will strengthen you, I will help you, I will uphold you with my righteous right hand." Does disciple making seem scary and hard? Fear not, for I am your God. Afraid of failure? God says to that fear, 'I will strengthen you and help you.'

2. Go therefore and make disciples of all nations

Here we see the command itself. I often focus on the 'therefore.' As the saying goes, "'If there is a therefore in Scripture, we ask, 'What is it there for?'" This 'therefore' is referencing the sentence before it:, 'All authority has been given to me.' Jesus is saying 'With this knowledge that as your Lord and Savior AND as the one commanding you to make disciples, go and make disciples, in your local area and around the world.'

---

5. Matthew 11:27

3.   Teaching them to observe all that I have commanded you

This is a largely untaught part of this passage. As we make disciples, we are also commanded to baptize those new disciples and teach them the things Jesus commands. Interesting, isn't it? We, as the ones commanded to make disciples, are commanded to also make sure the new disciples know about these commands and know how to obey them. This type of circular reasoning is right in line with Paul s admonition in 2 Timothy. The things you've heard me say and teach, entrust to reliable people, who will teach others. Commands that Jesus gives to us, we make sure to teach new disciples about the commands, with the heart they teach others also.

4. And behold, I am with you always, to the end of the age."

Finally, **remember this promise every day for the rest of your life.** As you memorize Matthew 28:18-20, don't skimp and leave this part of the passage out, which some have been in the habit of doing. Remember that Jesus is and will be with you. Jesus didn't abandon us when He hung on the cross and He won't leave us now as we go make disciples. His presence in your life and in the disciple making process provides a wonderful antidote for fear like nothing else can.

Authenticity and Accountability are Hard

As you start a disciple making relationship with another Christian, I must tell you that it's going to be hard. Hard for you. Hard for them. Hard all the way around. And it's going to be hard in part because as you begin to pick and probe into each other's lives, this accountability and authenticity are not seen in many of our other relationships and a lot of times, it feels unnatural. This creates obstacles that need to be addressed and solved! Allow me to break this down for you a bit, both to see why it's hard and what to do to make it a lot easier.

First, let's define some terms. Authenticity, that is, the quality of being authentic, is important in a disciple making relationship because if you and your disciplee are not being who you are normally, it's hard to get to the problems and sin issues that need to be exposed to the truth of the Gospel and healed in Christ. Quick example: If I'm unable to trust God because I have deep seated anger at my earthly father, and I don't talk about that in a disciple making relationship, it may stay unresolved for years. Or if the company CEO I'm discipling is committing adultery with his secretary and is hiding it from me, there's a big unresolved situation that affects both his own walk with Christ and his marriage, which clearly needs healing. It tends to be true that people's lives are messy and walking with them in a disciple making relationship will give us, and them, a backstage pass to the ugliness of their lives. And this may be an obstacle to someone coming into a relationship like this. The idea that they would willingly open themselves up to you in this way is a gap too wide for some.

Accountability then, is where the healing begins. It is where we take account of and responsibility for our actions. If I lied to my wife, I need to take responsibility for the lie, admit it to her, and be accountable to her to not do it again. In disciple making, having an accountability relationship with another person is really important. For example,: iIf I can't stop looking at pornography, but I know it's bad for my walk with Jesus and my marriage, I want to be a disciple of Jesus who is honoring God with my thoughts and my mind. The BEST way to do that is to have another person who is asking me weekly, 'Mike, I know you shared with me about your pornography problem, what did you do this week to find victory in that area?' This friend and I would define what 'victory' looks like in this area, and it may include a number of things. And because I know I'll have someone asking me, it's a reminder to be doing the things I need to be doing to find victory. You can enter into this example anything that you struggle with most. And by asking another person to be holding you accountable, this is a great growth area for the aspiring fully devoted follower of Jesus. As we read in Proverbs, "Iron sharpens iron, and one man sharpens another."[6] I need people in my life who are sharpening me toward being the disciple of Jesus I tell them I want to be.

So how do we navigate this issue and the potential obstacles they present? A couple of thoughts: First, I promise you that as you begin (if you haven't already started) to have a relationship with another Christian that has a high level of accountability and authenticity, you will see the growth in your walk with Christ. You will see how this type of relationship is critical to continuing in Christ. And you will then see how to communicate to a new disciplee why these aspects of your new relationship together are so critical. You'll be able to share from first-hand experience. The times I've grown the most in my walk with Christ, I've had someone holding me accountable and has 'kept it real' in my relationship with them. Secondly, as you begin getting into the messier side of each other's lives, always be sure to take whatever issue you're dealing with back to 'What does the Bible say about this?' Allow this to be your go-to response. Remember that "Tthe Wword of God is living and active, sharper than any two-edged sword, piercing to the division of soul and of spirit, of joints and of marrow, and discerning the thoughts and intentions of the heart."[7] What a powerful

---

6. Proverbs 27:17
7. Hebrews 4:12

verse! As we help a new disciple grow in Christ, spending as much time pouring over and memorizing God's Wword, this is a good thing. God's Wword does cut into the heart of what is really going on and it discerns the true thoughts and intentions of our hearts. I remember as a young Christian, one of my first jobs was at a car dealership. The manager of the dealership was asking me to be pretty dishonest with customers.[8] One of the first men to disciple me reminded me of 2 Corinthians 5:17, "Therefore, if anyone is in Christ, he is a new creation. The old has passed away; behold, the new has come." I didn't want to participate in these dishonest practices and was convicted through the Word of God, which led to me finding a job at a different dealership!

We Have an Enemy who Stands in Opposition

In our churches today, to me, it there doesn't seem to me to be enough education on the chief opponent of God and his influence in our world today. The Bible calls him the devil, Satan, and the evil one. Satan is a transliteration of a Hebrew word, which means "'adversary,'" or "'opponent.'" Painting with broad strokes, let's review who this enemy is and what authority he has here on earth and in our lives. As a created being,[9] he has dominion over the world and its system.[10] John states this clearly in 1 John, "We know that we are from God, and the whole world lies in the power of the evil one."[11] With his limited power, he actively works to nullify the effect of the Word of God in people's hearts[12] and he would then hate it for you to start meeting together with someone in a discipleship relationship. 1 Peter tells us that "Your adversary the devil prowls around like a roaring lion, seeking someone to devour."[13] We can assume that as God's enemy he wouldn't want people growing in their relationship with

8. As many car dealerships were back in the 1980's and 1990's
9. Exekiel 28:15
10. John 12:31
11. 1 John 5:19
12. Matthew 13:3-4,19
13. 1 Peter 5:8

Jesus, so you can also assume that there will be push back as you start discipling others. You'll find this pushback both in your life and in the lives of those you who start discipling. Because Satan cannot create anything, he tries to pervert, distort, and destroy what God has already created. In John 10, we read that "The thief comes only to steal and kill and destroy."[14] When we step out by faith to begin obeying Jesus' commands and pursuing people to join us in that pursuit, Satan will go after us and after our identity in Christ. How does he typically do this? Many times, he works through the opinions of others, through hurt and pain, and through the unrealistic expectations that media and culture place on us.

In this battle for our minds, Satan tries to put thoughts in our heads. We all know this battle as we have heard these attacks:

- 'I'm not good enough to earn God's acceptance and love'
- 'I'm not important to anyone'
- 'I'll never amount to anything....'
- 'Why would I think I could ever disciple someone else?'
- 'You know that sin you committed, you could never be forgiven for *that* one.'

If you begin hearing these types of accusations going through your mind, you know it's an attack of the enemy. And in the lives of those who we would want to disciple, in addition to the mental attacks I've just mentioned, we remember Paul's admonition in 2 Corinthians 4, "In their case the god of this world has blinded the minds of the unbelievers, to keep them from seeing the light of the gospel of the glory of Christ, who is the image of God."[15] While those you're hoping to disciple are not unbelievers, we see here that he is able to blind people from seeing the good of a life lives saturated by the light of the gospel. *Start meeting in a discipleship*

---

14. John 10:10
15. 2 Corinthians 4:3-4

relationship that enables me to live fully captivated by the Gospel? Why?

If any of this resonates with any of you, I have good news for you today. Through our relationship with Christ, we have the same victory that Christ has over this enemy! On the cross, Jesus secured victory over the enemy. I often remind myself and others of this wonderful passage from Colossians 2, one of the great passages of victory in the New Testament:

And you, who were dead in your trespasses and the uncircumcision of your flesh, God made alive together with him, having forgiven us all our trespasses, by canceling the record of debt that stood against us with its legal demands. This he set aside, nailing it to the cross. He disarmed the rulers and authorities and put them to open shame, by triumphing over them in him.[16]

While there's a lot packed into this passage, here's what I hope you will get out of this passage today. As you prepare to disciple another Christian, remember that the enemy has been disarmed and Christ, who you serve and who commands you to make disciples, has the ultimate triumph. Through Christ, we can bring the fullness of His work, on the cross, His resurrection and ascension against Satan and His work warring against you and your emerging disciple making ministry. Remember that "for he who is in you is greater than he who is in the world."[17]

Have Your Eyes Wide Open

As you enter into a disciple making ministry, remember Peter's admonition, "Be sober-minded; be watchful. Your adversary the devil prowls around like a roaring lion, seeking someone to devour. Resist him,

16. Colossians 2:14-15
17. 1 John 4:4

firm in your faith…"[18] Peter reminds us not only that the enemy is on the prowl, but that we should always 'be sober-minded' and to 'be watchful.' I've always found it interestinged that Peter's instruction would be to remain sober minded in relation to the enemy. The Greek word there translates to 'to be sober (not drunk), not intoxicated; free from illusion, i.e. from the intoxicating influences of sin.'[19] The way we can think of this for our modern minds would be to have presence of mind and clear judgement in relation to what our circumstances are in our current reality. I've found that when I am actively discipling someone and helping them grow, I find more weird and unusual things happening in my life. More strife at home and with friends than usual. The people I'm discipling are having a harder time making scheduled meeting times and completing the assignments I've given them to complete. None of this is happening by coincidence or by accident. Peter gives us a road map for why this these things are happening: We have an enemy, he is on the prowl, looking to devour, and our job is to be clear thinking and sober minded in order to see that there is a source for all of these problems.

Resist Him

Peter continues in his teaching that when we see these things happening, we're not called to sit idly by and allow these things to happen. We are called to resist him. I find the Greek word study helpful here as well, this time for the word resist. We would translate that word as 'to take a stand against and to hold your ground by taking a 180-degree position.' In the case I mentioned above, I would be called to dig deeper into the strife at home, looking for solutions and would talk openly to those I'm discipling about why they are having a hard time., and Iin all of this, I don't

---

18. 1 Peter 5:8-9
19. https://biblehub.com/greek/3525.htm

allow the devil's prowling to get me discouraged and downtrodden, but rather I call on the one who has the ultimate victory, and I refuse to allow the enemy to gain any ground. James tells us that as we resist the devil "he will flee from you."

Put on Your Armor, then Pray, Pray, Pray!

As Paul is ending his letter to the Ephesians, his last encouragement to them is to "be strong in the Lord and in his mighty power. Put on the full armor of God, so that you can take your stand against the devil's schemes."[20] This passage in Ephesians makes for a great study because there are six pieces of armor we are to gird ourselves with, and each has a specific purpose. It's encouraging to know that God's armor enables us to resist and take a stand against the enemy! As we 'armor up,' we are also pray, "praying at all times in the Spirit, with all prayer and supplication. To that end, keep alert with all perseverance, making supplication for all the saints…"[21] Prayer is an essential tool in disciple making. We pray for our own effectiveness in discipleship. We pray for those we want to ask to enter into a discipleship relationship. We then pray regularly for those who enter into this relationship, and we are regularly asking them how we can be praying for them and their lives. We pray for those who God may want to become disciple makers through our influence. We pray against the enemy and his schemes, both in our lives and in the lives of those we know. This is what it means to pray at all times. Everything gets bathed in prayer, and our prayer is the prayer of one who believes God is in control of all things and that His plan in all of this is the best plan.

As we pay attention to these obstacles with eyes wide open, we will find success in disciple making. And as I have said several times, as you

---

20. Ephesians 6:10-11
21. Ephesians 6:18

help more and more people toward spiritual formation, you'll get better at recognizing these obstacles and ways you've found to overcome them. In the next chapter, which is the final chapter of this book, I'm going to write about how long you should be meeting together with a particular person in a disciple making relationship. As we navigate this issue, you'll see that casting the vision to them about them their meeting with others leads to an 'off-boarding' process where you begin meeting less with them and cheering them on 'from the bleachers' as they disciple others. This is a crucial step in the disciple making process!

Let's finish strong!

Chapter 7

The 2 Timothy 2:2 Principle: Giving The Ministry Away

You then, my child, be strengthened by the grace that is in Christ Jesus, and what you have heard from me in the presence of many witnesses entrust to faithful men (people), who will be able to teach others also. -2 Timothy 2:1-2

For as long as humans have been on the earth, we've had a fascination with circles. This fascination predates recorded history, with many ancient cultures seeing the circle as a representation of the divine. In ancient Greece, it was seen as a sign of natural balance. The circle would later lead to one of the most important inventions of all time: the wheel. The invention of the wheel is largely thought of as the hallmark of human invention. From the invention of the wheel first came the potter's wheel, then the wheelbarrow, and later, when put together with the invention of the axel, wheels could then be used for transportation. Once humans didn't have to walk everywhere, everything changed! Of course, with the advent of serious advancements in materials, science has made possible all types of wheels and tires for bicycles, cars, motorcycles and trucks, all able to traverse many varied types of terrain. With all the wonderful accolades we heap on the circle, mathematicians state the 'the perfect circle' doesn't exist. For a circle to be perfect, we would need to measure an infinite number of points around the circle's circumference from the center to determine if it is actually perfect. Each point would need to be precisely equidistant from the center, which is essentially impossible to measure and quantify.

In disciple making, however, I believe the perfect circle does exist. As you've seen through the pages of this book, and as you become a fully devoted disciple of Jesus, you can form a perfect disciple making circle. As you carefully select 'F.A.T.' Christians who know part of your goal is to help them grow in their spiritual formation so that they can invest in other Christians in the same way, you can see the completion of 2 Timothy 2:1-2 in your life! I must say that there is almost not a better feeling of accomplishment I've had in my life than the times I've seen God help those I'm investing in develop a heart for discipling other people. And most of the time, this third ring of people were not people I knew before my disciplee mentioned their heart to help this 'third spiritual generation' in their own spiritual formation. Much like the process we see in a 4x100 relay race, where four 4 runners run 100 meters before passing on the baton to the next runner, thereby taking the baton one 1 full lap around the track, you too have the opportunity to pass the baton of disciple making to others who will then pass it on to yet others. In this final chapter, I'd like to help you form this perfect circle with tips and tools to help you transition your disciple making relationships to a relationship where they are discipling others, and you are transitioning your relationship from one of disciple maker/disciplee to more of a peer relationship. In this final chapter, there's some help I hope to give you on how long you should be meeting in a disciple making relationship and how to begin casting vision from the start for them to gain a heart to disciple others. We'll also look at the process of 'selective reproduction,' that which is the process of meeting less often to the point that you may only be meeting once or twice a year.

Finally, we'll look at, as you're not meeting together any longer on a regular basis, how you can continue to stay in touch and how you can encourage their journey from a distance.

Casting a Disciple Making Vision

The first step in passing the baton to those whom you've been discipling is to be casting a vision throughout the process of meeting together in disciple making. During the time you are meeting with your disciplee, being clear that the time you are spending with this other person is not only for the purpose of their spiritual formation, but it's also your heart to see the 2 Timothy 2:1-2 process play itself out, and that you're going to be teaching them in a way that they will be able to teach other people the same things. This goes to the intention side of what I've written about in Chapter 5. Making your intent clear from Day 1 is a great way for them to understand that you do not want this new relationship and what happens in it to stop with them. They then will know exactly what they are getting themselves into in this new relationship. As University of Houston professor Brené Brown often states, "Clear is kind. Unclear is unkind."[1] In disciple making specifically, if you fade into the 2 Timothy 2:1-2 process weeks after you've started, it's not nearly as easy for your disciplee to catch the vision and it's more likely that you will fade out of the relationship without someone who will be willing to receive the baton that you're trying to pass on to them.

So how do you prevent this fade? Habakkuk 2 gives us a good starting place. As Habakkuk was waiting to hear from God, we read, "And the LORD answered me: "Write the vision; make it plain on tablets, so he may run who reads it. For still the vision awaits its appointed time; it

---

1. https://brenebrown.com/articles/2018/10/15/clear-is-kind-unclear-is-unkind

hastens to the end—it will not lie. If it seems slow, wait for it; it will surely come; it will not delay."[2] Although we may not physically write down 2 Timothy 2:1-2, pass the baton vision and hand it to them, we certainly want to write that vision down on their hearts by mentioning your heart to see them teaching others from the beginning. Talk about it with them often and ask them a month or two into your meeting together to begin praying about who they could begin meeting with in the same way you're meeting with them. As you two pray together, begin praying with them about those who God may have in store for them to pass the baton on to. In addition, your personal commitment to and track record in being able to receive the baton and pass on to them will speak volumes. And finally, as we see in Habakkuk 2, it may take some time for the vision to be fully maturated in their lives and in their hearts. As we read in this chapter of Habakkuk, "If it seems slow, wait for it; it will surely come: it will not delay." This is where you can trust God and be praying for them to catch this vision and begin speaking about it on their own. In my own disciple making journey, I love seeing how God works through the casting of vision into the lives of those I've invested in. It's truly supernatural!

How Long Should You Keep Meeting Together?

As you meet together with your disciplee, the question of 'How long you should meet together?' is a complex question to answer. I start our thinking through the answer to this question in two directions: As I mentioned in Chapter 4 in the section about selection, it's important to select a Faithful, Available and Teachable person to begin discipling. There are times that, as you're meeting on regular intervals with someone that you previously thought was Faithful, Available and Teachable, you find that

---

2. Habakkuk 2:1-3

they are not Faithful, Available, or Teachable, and you have to decide what to do in this relationship. This is a difficult situation, because, I've found myself beating myself up mentally since it seemed like my ability to discern about the person was off. 'What was I thinking,' I may think to myself. 'What do I do now?' If you find yourself in this type of situation, please don't be too hard on yourself and allow me to say to you that this type of situation can and does happen. It's OK. At this point, it's time to make an assessment, because if they are not actually ready, they're not ready, and it's not your fault. Maybe it turns out to be a bad season for them, or maybe because they are not either Faithful, Available and Teachable, it would be time to have a chat with them and let them know that, in hindsight, you don't think they are ready, and you'd love to keep a relationship with them, seeing each other a few times a year for coffee. This type of chat can be good for you and good for them. I've found it to be good for me, because I only have a certain amount of time to meet with people, and this gives me the time back to invest in someone else who may be ready. And it could be good for them because they will probably end up not doing the things that need to be done for them to grow spiritually in the ways you're hoping they will. And as I mentioned in Chapter 4, making this assessment doesn't mean that there is anything wrong with them, and as you move them to an 'I'm going to be praying for you' mode, you hopefully will see God work in some ways in their life that would make them ready in the future. And because you've put the disciple making part of your relationship with them on the back burner, you can just as easily put it back on the front burner. This will enable you all to pick up where you left off when it's a better season or they are in a better place spiritually. No harm, no foul!

The second scenario you'll find is someone who has been completely Faithful, and Available, and Teachable, and is catching the vision of taking the 2 Timothy 2:1-2 baton from you and has been praying about who God would want them to begin investing in. I love it when people I'm investing in get to this point! Obviously, the first step here is to be praying often with them and without them about this process of their own selection. You can also be teaching them about selection and what you've learned, even if they are your first people that you've discipled. You now technically have experience in disciple making! And in relation to when to begin the process of meeting less often, this is a bit of a judgement call. I would think that you would first want to at least go through the 24 weekly topics found in the resources section, plus any other topics God has put on your heart to teach them about. A little mathematics helps us here: 24 weeks is a little over 5 ½ months, so let's say that you also have six other topics of your own choosing you'd like to teach them, so now we're at a little under seven months. And if you've missed a couple of weeks together because of scheduling problems and you have a holiday or two that has crept in, you can see that you're beginning to approach eight months. This is a good exercise because in terms of intentionality, if you know going in that you have eight months with this person, the questions of 'What would I want them to know in the eight months we're together weekly?' provides some intentionality. Think through the answer to this question strategically when you start meeting with them. The hope would be that as you all approach six months or so, they are beginning to see some people that they are feeling led to invest in themselves, and you can be praying for them and as you finish your eight months of teaching, you can begin to transition your conversation toward their own selection and the preparation they need to begin meeting with others. In talking about this recently with the man who originally discipled me 30 years ago, he mentioned that he's found it generally takes longer than you think. His recommendation was to not be afraid if it's 18 months until those you disciple seem ready to begin helping another person grow spiritually.

Having been in full-time ministry for a long time, I've seen this process of giving away disciple making ministry done well and done not so well. If you've been in ministry long enough, you begin to see all types of effective and ineffective ministry. One of the dangers we all need to avoid is thinking that we're the only ones who can do a particular work with a particular person. I remember when I was first in full-time ministry, serving with The Navigators at Colorado State University. Over the years, I got to know the other campus ministers and I began to hear a similar phrase when we campus ministers would all come together for fellowship. This phrase of 'my people' came up a lot, as in 'Yeah, I have a lot going on with my people.' The meaning of 'my people' was the people who I'm ministering to, but it clearly came across as 'I'm the only one who can minister to these people.' It's easy for us to get in a trap of pride as we minister to others, thinking that we hold some special power with our people. I think a better phrase would be, 'It's great to see what's happening with the people God has given us.' 'God's people' lines up biblically a lot better than 'my people.' The Apostle Paul echoes this sentiment as he writes, "What then is Apollos? What is Paul? Servants through whom you believed, as the Lord assigned to each. I planted, Apollos watered, but God gave the growth. So neither he who plants nor he who waters is anything, but only God who gives the growth. He who plants and he who waters are one, and each will receive his wages according to his labor."[3] God is clearly

---

3. 1 Corinthians 3:5-8

the one doing the work in whomever we may disciple, and we mustn't fall for the trap of self-promotion. Paul hits the nail on the head as he wrote to the Roman church, "For by the grace given to me I say to everyone among you not to think of himself more highly than he ought to think, but to think with sober judgment, each according to the measure of faith that God has assigned."[4] As we enter into disciple making ministry, we must always remember the example of Jesus. In John 21, we see Jesus ask Peter three times to feed his sheep and tend to the pasture. In one of the last of Jesus' post-resurrection appearances to His disciples on the shores of the Sea of Galilee, Jesus makes one more appeal to Peter to take over the ministry that Jesus had carefully crafted. We must be eager to trust God with those He's entrusting us with, knowing that it's His working in those we've discipled to then be used to minister to others. Stepping aside, letting go and letting God work is very important as we begin the process of selective reproduction.

Finally, it's important to have some metrics around when someone you are discipling is ready to disciple others. It would be a disservice to your disciplee to send them out too soon, like a junior mechanic not ready to rebuild their first transmission. They have some of the tools because they are a mechanic, but maybe not the technical skills. I'm going to recommend 5 metrics for you to use to make sure your disciplee is ready to begin discipling others.

4. Romans 12:3

5 Metrics For Someone To Disciple Another

6 Marks of a Disciple

In Chapter 2, as I was helping you make sure you were ready to make disciples, I gave you 6 Marks of a Disciple from my book *What You Do Shows Who You Are: The 6 Marks of a Disciple of Jesus.*[5] Since I recommended these 6 Marks for you, I would also recommend that you use them as a way to determine if those you are discipling are ready to make disciples themselves. The 'magic' of these 6 Marks is that new believers around the world have often told me that they 'hit the mark' when it comes to knowing the key things that a disciple is and does. Going through the book with your disciplee as a first step is never a bad idea. You could then go from that book to the 24 weekly topics found in the resources section of this book. In particular, you want to see if your disciplee exemplifies these 6 Marks in their lives and that you can see these 6 Marks have taken root and are true in their lives.

Can Confidently Share Their Testimony and the Gospel

Because Jesus calls us all to proclaim the Gospel and make disciples, you will want anyone you're discipling to know how to share the story of how they came to Christ and have a clear presentation of what is the Gospel. This is definitely a metric you'll want to have, both for yourself and for those you are discipling. The reason I think both of these are so important is because if you can't tell the story of how you came to Christ and know the details of the Gospel, you're not ready to begin making disciples. There are many online tools where you can learn these important skills. As an example, the organization where I serve, One Eight Catalyst,

5. The complete book is available on Amazon.com.

we've created a training website, EquippingDepot.org. At this site, we have online training courses on both How to Share Your Testimony and How to Share the Gospel. This is just one of many places where this content is available.

Handles the Word Correctly

In 2 Timothy, as Paul details his metrics for what he wanted for Timothy to know, he wrote, "Do your best to present yourself to God as one approved, a worker who has no need to be ashamed, rightly handling the word of truth."[6] In order for this instruction to be true in our lives, we must know God's Word and be able to teach from it accurately and without falsehoods. Knowing God's Word and being able to accurately teach from it will garner God's approval. As I've said about my own teaching ministry, I am always trying to be 'dead on' when it comes to teaching and preaching, and I've found in my own life that this is done both by spending regular time in God's Word and by taking the time to study the passages that I'm going to be teaching on.

Shows An Understanding and Application To The 24 Weekly Topics

As to the 24 weekly topics, they are given as a guide for you to use as you disciple and teach your new disciplees. I would hope that you and your disciplees not only understand them but would internalize them and make them your own. To be able to fully internalize topics like 'Victory over Sin' and 'Lordship of Christ' means that you not only understand it, but also believe the teaching to be true and are now living differently because of the Biblical truth you studied. This is important for the disciplee as they begin praying about disciple making because if they are not living

6. 2 Timothy 2:15

differently because of this teaching, they won't be able to teach it to others. I have a long-standing belief that it's our stated beliefs, together with our actual practice, that determines our actual beliefs. This is very true here as a metric toward being ready to make disciples.

Shows a Love for Scripture Memory

Maybe it's my Navigators background and training, but I have always wanted someone who is making disciples to be one who has a heart for Scripture memory. In several places in this book, I proclaim my love of memorization of God's Word, so I won't do that here. Suffice it to say that when you've hidden God's Word in your heart, you're quite equipped to give biblical counsel and can 'pull up' Scripture that fits whatever conversation you're having with those you're discipling. Remember that it's really God who makes disciples and we're called to equip ourselves to be involved however He sees fit.

Selective Reproduction: The Process of Meeting Less Often

As we begin to look at meeting with those whom we've been discipling less often, and we talk through how to accomplish that successfully, let's remember that one of our goals is to join together with those we've discipled to make more disciples. In the case of the church or ministry leader, as we disciple others, they people are added to the number of those who want to make more disciples. If you remember my example of multiplication, as you and your disciplee each get a new person to disciple, you've gone from two people to four people, which turns grows to 8, then 16 and so on. While you may not be meeting with that first disciplee as often, you'll be going through the process of selective reproduction, that is, as people meet your metrics and you all start meeting with new people, you will see a new ministry starting as you train others to do what you've been called to do.

As those you've been discipling are ready, that is, they meet the metrics you've set and have been through the process of intentionally inviting others to begin meeting with them in a disciple making relationship, you'll begin meeting with these original disciplees less often. This may be once a month, four times a year... whatever timing you all set up together. These meetings can be a wonderful time for you to do a 'check in' on how they are doing in their walk with Jesus and how the early days of disciple making are treating them. You are now in the role of 'disciple making adviser' as they begin meeting with their new disciplees, and they request help as they start discipling another Christian. I always enjoy these meetings because as they go out 'into the battle' of disciple making, we come back together, and I can encourage them in what they are doing and provide advice in areas where they are struggling. And if you remember me mentioning earlier in this book, there's nothing easy about disciple making, and being able to encourage and help is a huge deal. Practically, if you were meeting weekly with your disciplee, you all may agree to begin meeting once or twice a month, depending on the felt needs of your disciplee. Be sure to communicate that although you two will be meeting less frequently, your heart for them, their walk for Christ and their future ministry will never wane. I remember the first time I began discipling others, these meetings with the man discipling me were lifesavers because many times it felt like I had no idea what I was doing, and to be able to have someone to ask things like, 'So Billy, who I'm meeting with, is struggling with pornography, what do I do about that?' or 'He doesn't seem to get this idea of being fully identified with Christ. What passages should I take him through?' To have someone to search the Scriptures with and pray together for Billy was everything. As an important side note, this stage is an important part of the overall disciple making process in the lives of those whom you'll invest in. Not only are they learning to trust God's direction in discipleship, but you as a disciple maker want these initial disciple making ventures of those you've invested in to go well. It'll set them up either as a disciple maker for life, or as someone who tried it once and burned out because it didn't go well. This reminds me of what I've heard over the years about Bill Walton, the Hall of Fame basketball player of the 1970's and 1980's. While Walton was a good scorer, he was an expert in passing and getting the basketball to his teammates into a good position to score. If you've done your job in disciple making, you'll set up well those you've invested in to 'score' in their own ministry, while you cheer them on from the bleachers.

Intentional Disengagement: Cheering from the Bleachers

The last stage of selective reproduction in discipleship is completely up to you and your disciplee. Over the years, if you are faithful in disciple making and gain an increasing amount of people that you've discipled, you may find it hard to meet with all of them even once a month. But because you've spent quality time with these people, you don't want the relationship to end as it becomes more of a peer-to-peer friendship, where they are making disciples like are you, and you'll want them to know you're in their corner no matter what. Because you all have become friends, you may want to see each other a couple times a year for a dinner or to catch a ball game together. My hope for you in these relationships would be that these people would be some of the strongest, longest lasting friendships you have. I hope these friendships match Jesus' hope for us as we develop strong friendships, "This is my commandment, that you love one another as I have loved you. Greater love has no one than this, that someone lay down his life for his friends."[7] If you all are going to the same church, you may continue to see each other regularly, and will commit to a twice-a-year dinner with extended family as a point of fellowship and reconnection. It'll be a great honor for you to be able to look back years from now and see all the people God has given you to disciple and how many people God gave those you helped with in their spiritual formation! This is where you'll see the multiplication principles I mentioned in the Introduction coming to life! Even if you had one person a year you were discipling and that one person a year discipled one person a year, you will be able to see the impact you are having! This would mean hundreds of people every ten years that you commit to disciple making, all of whom have a heart to both obey Christ's commands and want to see others become fully devoted disciples of Jesus.

Final Thoughts

Thank you so much for coming with me on this disciple making journey. I have truly taught you everything I can think of for you to begin making disciples. While there are other books that get into much greater detail regarding disciple making, I find many of those volumes lacking in relation to the 'nitty gritty' of walking the reader through the step-by-step process of how to actually make disciples. In the resources section, I'll mention these other volumes and by reading them, you'll certainly add to your understanding from other author's' perspectives. As I hope you've

7. John 15:12-13

seen by reading through my book, now you can truly begin making disciples! You'll be counted as one who reads the command Jesus gives to make disciples and are obeying it! My advice to you is start with just one person. Grab a person you've already known at church or in a Bible Study you are already attending. This person may be very familiar to you, which will make your first journey into disciple making a little easier. And along the way, always remember that it's God that makes disciples. You are just a vessel that God chooses to use! Then, a year from now, invite another person, or maybe you'll feel bold enough to invite two people to meet with you, where you can meet all together! Sometimes, the dynamic of three or four people all meeting together has its advantages. After you've 'gotten your feet wet,' continue to pray for more opportunities. I have a friend, for example, who discipled three people at his church, and the leaders of the church noticed what he was doing and asked him to lead a class on how to make disciples, just from the example he set that he was serious about disciple making. God may open up additional doors for you to teach this content overseas. You never know what God may want to do, but it sure seems to me that you have to start with that one person and pray that God will use you in mighty ways. As the great ice hockey player great Wayne Gretzky said, "You miss 100% of the shots you don't take." If you don't 'take a shot' at inviting one person to join you in disciple making, you'll never see how God may want to use you in the future.

I'm so thankful that you've read this book. I'll be praying that God will use you in mighty ways and if there's ever anything I can do to encourage you along the way, please don't hesitate to reach out. May God bless you in your disciple making journey, and may you impact hundreds

Disciple Making Resources

In this section, you'll find all the resources that I have mentioned throughout the book. Being the President and Founder of a ministry that creates resources and delivers training, I love good resources! I think that, especially for disciple making, you can't have enough good resources, handouts and video courses. Please feel free to use these resources freely! I'm hopeful that they will add to your ability to make disciples that make disciples.

I've created these for you to be a better disciple maker and I hope you find that they meet this mark. On one hand, everything I think you'll need is in this section and on the other hand, I held back anything that wasn't going to be of use to you as a new disciple maker. And while I wish that I could be there with you to help you in your disciple making journey (especially those of you who are at it for the first time!), I offer these resources as a hope that they may help you make disciples! Praying for all who use these resources.

120

Weekly Bible Study Topics

As you've read in multiple places within the book, as you begin meeting with your new disciplee, I've wanted to give you the initial topics for you to cover as you begin helping them in their spiritual growth and formation. For each topic, there are six section for you to cover. In other disciple making books I've used in the past, one of them has had a section similar to this, but I always felt like I wished there was more information.

One other note before I explain each of the six sections: A couple of people who proofread the book before publication recommended that in addition to the format I've given you here, that I consider a separate handout for each topic that could be downloaded from the internet. While I appreciated the heart behind their suggestion, I decided not to do that for a specific reason. In going through these topics with people that I've discipled, there is a great dynamic of me teaching the content to them, and them hearing the information for the first time. They learn how to take notes, making in essence what is a handout of their own. Hearing the content from me for the first time enables them to be really taking the content in, thereby increasing retention and engagement with the content.

Because I want you to be able to use this content to it's fullest, let me briefly go through the six topics, explaining what each of them are and what you'll be looking for in terms of teaching it to others.

Each weekly topic has six sections. Here's a brief overview of each of the sections:

Why is this Topic Important?

You'll find the information here going in two ways: Obviously, I do want to tell you why the topic for the week is important, but also I want to give a bit of a definition of the topic. Please don't hesitate as you are preparing to teach this content to another person to do additional research about the topic, mainly for your own understanding.

Practical Application Points

This is the list of what to do as you're going through the topic with another. You'll see things like 'Talk to them about _____' or 'Ask them to give you their understanding of _____.' This literally is your list of what to do as you have your weekly time with them.

Scripture Verses on the Topic

I've given you four Scripture verses to go through with them as you discern what the Bible has to say about a particular topic. If you already know of or find addition Scripture verses that deal directly with the topic, feel free to use them as well. I have a heart to have the Bible speak about these topics, so be sure to go through the verses to allow the Bible to speak.

Desired Outcome from the Application

In this section, I'm giving you a 'Here's where you want to be after teaching' on the topic. Sometimes, you might find that it takes a couple of weeks for them to really grasp what you're teaching on. To that I would say: Take the two weeks and know that the end result is both an understanding of the topic AND a changed life because of what God is doing because of the information.

Other Helpful Resources

If they are available, I've put additional resources that may help you understand and teach the topic to them. This is your 'homework' section, based on your interest in diving into further understanding of the topic.

Optional Scripture Memory Verses

As you've read in a couple of places, I'm a big fan of Scripture memory and believe it is one of the best tools for you to use with your disciplee. I think Psalm 119, verses 9 and 11 sum up best my thoughts on Scripture memory, "How can a young man keep his way pure? By guarding it according to your word. I have stored up your word in my heart, that I might not sin against you." It is completely true that as a way to combat sin and keep our eyes focused on God, storing up God's word in our hearts is a wonderful way to do that! In the Resources section of this book, you'll find a two-page 'how-to' to help you get started on Scripture memory. In the weekly schedule with your disciplee, it's an easy 7 minutes to add to quiz each other on your Scripture memory verses you've been working on during the week. It is also a way to see how faithful they are at doing what you are asking them to do. A disciplee who comes not ready to recite their verses may not be as faithful as they seem.

Week 1

Assurance of Salvation

Why is this Topic Important?

Quite obviously, we want anyone we're discipling to know for sure that they are saved. Many times, Christians look for assurance of their salvation in the wrong places. As you go through the Scripture verses together, you'll see that salvation is found in Christ alone. This topic is important because we don't want our disciplees to lives out their lives unsure of their salvation.

Practical Application Points

1. Have them share their testimony with you about how they became a Christian.

2. If there seems to be any 'gaps,' meaning if they missed some spots, go over with them the gospel message again.

3. Over time, observe how they explain their conversion experience with others.

Scripture Verses on the Topic

John 1:12-13

John 5:24

1 John 5:11-13

Romans 8:16

Desired Outcome from the Application
        You want them to be able to express with confidence to others their own assurance of salvation based on their own personal faith, using Scripture as their guide.

Other Helpful Resources
John MacArthur Video on YouTube:
https://www.youtube.com/watch?v=Mi53UwZ5br0
Great explanation on gotquestions.org:
https://www.gotquestions.org/assurance-salvation.html

Optional Scripture Memory Verses
John 5:24
1 John 5:13

Week 2

Bible Reading and Study

Why is this Topic Important?

Bible Reading and Study is important because the Bible is the very Word of God. If you want to know God's will, start reading your Bible! I can't tell you how many times God has directed me to do a certain thing or go in a certain direction through time in His Word. In addition, having a deeper understanding of the Bible helps us know the nature of God and how our lives connect to His redemptive plan laid out throughout Scripture.

Practical Application Points

1. Talk about how they are currently reading God's word and set up with them a plan to read God's word daily.

2. Share with them what it is that you've found helping in doing Bible study.

3. Talk about the difference between Bible reading and Bible study.

Scripture Verses on the Topic

Proverbs 2:1-5

2 Timothy 3:16-17

Hebrews 4:12

Acts 17:11

Desired Outcome from the Application

You want to instill in them a heart to become students of God's word, both through daily reading and regular times of study.

Other Helpful Resources

The Navigators Word Hand Illustration:

https://www.navigators.org/resource/the-word-hand/

Easy to Follow Bible Reading Plan: http://oneeightcatalyst.org/wp-content/uploads/2019/12/OEC-5-Day-Bible-Plan.pdf

Optional Scripture Memory Verses

2 Timothy 3:16-17

Hebrews 4:12

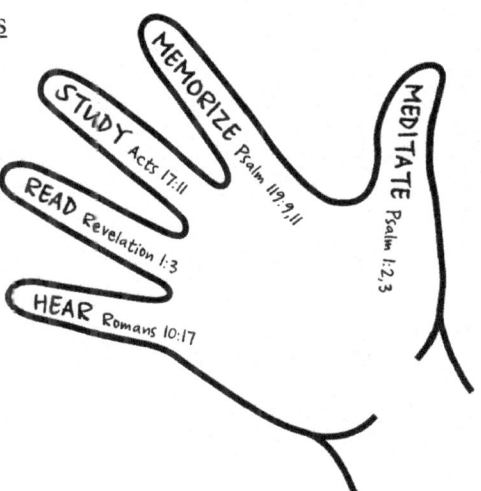

The Navigators Word Hand

Week 3

Scripture Memory

Why is this Topic Important?

There is almost no spiritual discipline that has meant more to my walk with Christ than Scripture memory. If you and the people you disciple can get into the habit of regular Scripture memory, it will 'rise the tide' of your walk with Christ and those who you are discipling. Not only will it help in your walk with Christ, it also increases your understanding and knowledge of Scripture. It also is a great ward against sin and a propellant toward Godly living. As we read in Psalm 119, "I have stored up your word in my heart, that I might not sin against you."

Practical Application Points

1. Go through the 'How to Begin Memorizing Scripture' worksheet, found in the Resources Section on page 172

2. Explain to them the personal blessing you've found in memorizing Scripture

3. Develop a plan to begin quizzing each other each week as you memorize the verses provided for each weekly topic

Scripture Verses on the Topic

Matthew 4:4

Psalm 1:1-3

Colossians 3:16

Deuteronomy 6:6-9

Desired Outcome from the Application

For yourself and those you disciple, being able to maintain a weekly habit of memorizing Scripture and being able to review past verses, would be a great outcome!

Other Helpful Resources

Learning How to do Scripture Memory Resource Sheet on Page 173

The Navigators Topical Memory System:

https://www.navigators.org/resource/topical-memory-system/

Scripture Memory App for Smartphones: https://www.remem.me

Optional Scripture Memory Verses

Psalm 119:9-11

Joshua 1:8

Week 4

Prayer

Why is this Topic Important?

Simply put, for disciples of Jesus prayer is the best way to communicate with God. It is the vehicle for daily dialogue with the One who created us. It cannot be overestimated the importance of daily communication with God through prayer. This opportunity we have daily to share all the aspects of our lives with God is so important that it's mentioned over 250 times in the Bible. As we pray daily, we have the opportunity to both express our gratitude and confess and ask for help in overcoming our sin.

Practical Application Points

1. Ask them to share some answers to prayer and share with them some answers you've received.

2. As you do the Scripture study on prayer, focus on ways that the Bible indicates we should we be praying.

3. Make opportunities to pray together, both individually and in a group setting.

4. Make a plan to share prayer requests with each other, and review those week after week, seeing how God works through prayer.

Scripture Verses on the Topic

1 Thessalonians 5:16-18

Matthew 6:6

James 5:16

1 John 5:14

Desired Outcome from the Application

We would want them to know the importance of prayer, that it is a direct 'pipeline' to be able to talk to God. Also, it would be great if they would see pray as a regular and constant part of their lives, that praying is normative, both individually and corporately.

Other Helpful Resources

Starting a Prayer Journal can be a great way to record and organize prayer requests. A simple journal can be found at many stores.

PrayerMate helps you pray consistently for people and develop a discipline of prayer: prayermate.net/app

Optional Scripture Memory Verses

John 15:7

Philippians 4:6-7

Week 5

Quiet Time

Why is this Topic Important?

This time that is often called by Christians a 'quiet time' is dedicated one-on-one time with God and His Word. This daily time with God is important because it gives us the opportunity to set our minds on God to begin the day and the routine of daily time in prayer and God's word is a wonderful spiritual discipline toward growth.

Practical Application Points

1. Talk through what they are already doing in terms of a daily Quiet Time.

2. Describe to them the blessings and growth you've seen by doing your daily Quiet Time.

3. If they are not having a Quiet Time, help them develop a plan towards this end. An easy starting point is to have a 30-minute Quiet Time: 10 minutes in prayer, 10 minutes reading a Bible passage, and 10 minutes praying for concerns in their lives.

Scripture Verses on the Topic

Mark 1:35

Genesis 19:27

1 Samuel 1:19

1 Corinthians 1:9

Desired Outcome from the Application

You're hoping that if they are not having a regular Quiet Time, that they will see the need and begin spending time daily in prayer and God's word. As they start that daily time with God, you're also hoping and praying that God would speak to them and use that time toward their spiritual formation.

Other Helpful Resources

The Navigators have a great online resource that gets you started on structuring a regular Quiet Time:

https://www.navigators.org/resource/daily-quiet-time/

The You Version App is a Bible app that has many included (and free!) resources, from Bible Reading plans to devotionals, all available on your smartphone.

Optional Scripture Memory Verses

Mark 1:35

1 Corinthians 1:9

Week 6

Victory Over Sin

Why is this Topic Important?

As previously written about in this book, we have an enemy who would love for us to not find victory over sin in our lives. We have a Christ, however, that has found final victory of death and over this enemy. Through the Holy Spirit we can be victorious in our lives in Christ over sin.

Practical Application Points

1. Talk about a recent victory you've had over sin and how you saw God take you through that experience.

2. As you read through the Scripture verses, spend a little extra time doing a study together of 1 Corinthians 10:13.

3. Develop a plan to be accountable to one another to confess when each person is struggling with sin. As it becomes 'out in the open,' you both can be praying for one another that Jesus would enable you to have victory over that sin.

Scripture Verses on the Topic

1 Corinthians 10:13
1 Corinthians 15:57
Isaiah 41:13
1 John 1:7-10

Desired Outcome from the Application

Your goal here is to see your disciplee experience victory over temptation and sin through a reliance on the Holy Spirit and trusting the promises found in the Bible.

Other Helpful Resources

GotQuestions.org has a great overview:
https://www.gotquestions.org/victory-over-sin.html

Optional Scripture Memory Verses

1 Corinthians 10:13
1 John 1:9

Week 7

Christian Fellowship

Why is this Topic Important?
      Fellowship with other Christians is one of the essentials of the faith. These relationships of mutual benefit between Christians are important for the person who wants to walk with Jesus. These relationships with other believers in Jesus are important for several reasons: There is a unity amongst believers that provides encouragement, support and accountability in our lives. Because Christians are united together in the Holy Spirit through our shared relationship with Jesus, we play an important role in each other's lives.

Practical Application Points
   1. Talk together about their church background and their thoughts about the importance of fellowship with other believers.
   2. See what small groups and/or Sunday School classes they are already involved in.
   3. If they don't yet have a church home, help them strategically think through how to find a church home.

Scripture Verses on the Topic
Acts 2:42
1 John 1:3
Hebrews 10:24-25
Psalm 122:1

Desired Outcome from the Application

Any person that you disciple, you want them to be active in a local church and have Bible studies and small group ministry to be involved in.

Other Helpful Resources

A simple Google search can help find local churches in the area. Be sure to find a church that teaches from God's word and has a heart toward Great Commission fulfillment.

Optional Scripture Memory Verses
Matthew 18:20
Hebrews 10:24-25

Week 8

Biblical Authority

Why is this Topic Important?

The Bible says of itself that it is the authoritative word of God. In fact, in 2 Timothy 2:2, Paul writes that "all Scripture is breathed out by God and profitable for teaching, for reproof, for correction, and for training in righteousness." The disciple of Jesus must have confidence in God's Word as an authoritative text that God has inspired and ordained. If the disciple wants to know God and hear from God, that communication happens primarily through the Bible. This disciple knows that God saves by the Bible, He sanctifies by the Bible, and He comforts, edifies and does all spiritual work by the Bible. The foundation of all Christian endeavor is the Word of God.

Practical Application Points

1. Talk about their understanding of the authority of the Bible and how that applies in their lives.

2. Make a correlation between spending time reading the Bible and turning that gained knowledge into personal action.

3. Have a discussion about how important it is for the Christian to be 'If the Bible says it, we'll do it' people and how you both can become those types of people.

Scripture Verses on the Topic
2 Timothy 3:16-17
Hebrews 4:12
John 17:8
1 Thessalonians 2:13

Desired Outcome from the Application

I think there are two main desired outcomes during this time together. Because fewer and fewer people believe that the Bible is the authoritative word of God, making sure that point is made is crucial. If we believe that God has all authority and the Bible is the word of God, it too has full authority. It's hard for a Christian to live a victorious life in Christ and have doubt about the Bible. Secondly, the belief about the authority of the Bible translates to so many other weekly topics here. Why memorize Scripture if it's not the Word of God? Why read the Bible daily? Taking that understanding of the Bible and then applying what we read from the Bible is really important as well.

Other Helpful Resources

A Google search on Biblical archeology is one of my favorite places to go. Seeing how the archeology matches what we read in the Bible lends credence to its authority.
Cru has a great article about the Authority of the Bible:
https://www.cru.org/us/en/train-and-grow/spiritual-growth/the-authority-of-scripture.html

Optional Scripture Memory Verses
2 Timothy 3:16-17
Hebrews 4:12

Week 9

Personal Testimony

Why is this Topic Important?

A personal testimony is simply the story of how you came to receive and believe in Jesus, and it's often a first step towards sharing the Gospel. It's important because a Christian who cannot share the story of how they became a Christian should immediately shore that up in their lives. 1 Peter 3:15 is one of my favorite verses in this area, "but in your hearts honor Christ the Lord as holy, always being prepared to make a defense to anyone who asks you for a reason for the hope that is in you; yet do it with gentleness and respect." We as Christians should always be able to give anyone who asks us the reason for the hope we have in Christ.

Practical Application Points

1. Share your personal testimony with them.

2. Have them share their personal testimony with you.

3. Do a brief Bible study together of Acts 26:1-23 noting Paul's approach to his testimony.

Scripture Verses on the Topic

1 Peter 3:15

Luke 8:38-39

Colossians 4:5-6

1 John 1:3

Desired Outcome from the Application

You want to have at least two outcomes from this time together. First, making sure that they can easily tell the story of how they came to Jesus is important. Secondly, being able to tie it together with opportunities to share the Gospel with others is key. Testimony telling and sharing the Gospel are equal in importance.

Other Helpful Resources

One Eight Catalyst has a equipping website at EquippingDepot.org. For anyone who does not know how to share their testimony, we have an online video course on how to share your testimony, complete with a two page worksheet. You may need to take extra weeks to go through this course together, practicing and perfecting their personal testimony.

Optional Scripture Memory Verses

1 Peter 3:15

Colossians 4:5-6

Week 10

Sharing The Gospel

Why is this Topic Important?

Sharing the Gospel is among the most important of these 24 topics simply because Jesus gave us the command in Mark 16 to proclaim the Gospel. We are the primary vehicle for those without Christ to know about Jesus and have the opportunity to receive Him as Lord. From a discipleship view, making sure your disciplee knows how to share the Gospel is important, not only because Jesus commands us to do it, but also because it is when we can easily share the Gospel that we understand and internalize it into our own lives.

Practical Application Points

1. Have them share the Gospel with you according to their current understanding.

2. If they have gaps in being able to share the Gospel, go through the EquippingDepot.org course together on how to share the Gospel using the Three Circles method.

3. Make opportunities to share the Gospel with them.

4. Be praying together for opportunities to share the Gospel, making a list of those you're praying for and follow through by sharing the Gospel with those people.

Scripture Verses on the Topic
Colossians 1:28-29
2 Timothy 4:1-2
Acts 8:35
1 Corinthians 15:3-4

Desired Outcome from the Application

Obviously, you'll want them to be able to share the Gospel clearly and easily. I emphasize this with those I've discipled because someone who can clearly and easily share the Gospel has internalized it's meaning and is not ashamed of the Gospel. Also, you'll be working together on a growing heart for the lost, understanding that those without Christ are eternally separated from God. A disciple of Jesus wants everyone to have this story for their eternity.

Other Helpful Resources

One Eight Catalyst has a equipping website at EquippingDepot.org. For anyone who does not know how to share the Gospel, we have a online video course on how to share the Gospel, complete with a two page worksheet. You may need to take extra weeks to go through this course together, practicing and perfecting how to share the Gospel.

Optional Scripture Memory Verses
Matthew 4:19
Romans 1:16

Week 11

Lordship of Christ

Why is this Topic Important?

The doctrine of Christ's lordship is a foundational truth of the Christian faith. The truth that Jesus Christ is our Lord, that is, that He is our master and has full authority is crucial for the disciple of Jesus. Paul illustrates this well in 2 Corinthians 4:5 as He writes, "For what we proclaim is not ourselves, but Jesus Christ as Lord, with ourselves as your servants for Jesus' sake." He is Lord and we serve Him and look to Him as our master.

Practical Application Points

1. Begin a conversation about their understanding of the Lordship of Christ.

2.Do a Bible study together on Colossians 1:18 and Hebrews 1 together.

Scripture Verses on the Topic

Romans 12:1-2

Colossians 1:18

Hebrews 1:2

2 Corinthians 4:5

Desired Outcome from the Application

You'd love to see a lordship commitment by allowing Christ to control areas of their lives previously not under the lordship of Christ, and a greater understand of how having Christ as Lord of their lives affects and influences all areas of their life.

Other Helpful Resources

For a very thorough look at this topic, I'll recommend Vern Poythress' book The Lordship of Christ: Serving Our Savior All of the Time, in All of Life, with All of Our Heart.

Optional Scripture Memory Verses

Romans 12:1-2

2 Corinthians 4:5

Week 12

Trusting God By Faith

Why is this Topic Important?

This is an important topic because trusting God is essential as an element of a saving faith that looks to God for peace, contentment and strength. And trusting God by faith is key here: In Hebrews 11:6, we read that "without faith it is impossible to please him, for whoever would draw near to God must believe that he exists and that he rewards those who seek him." Trusting God by faith is important because as Christians, we must believe in his existence and in all that he has done, is doing, and will do, both now and forever in his Son Jesus Christ.

Practical Application Points

1. Talk about their understanding of trusting God by faith.

2. Do a simple Bible Study together on Hebrews 11:1-6.

3. Encourage them to look at areas that they can trust God by faith in deeper ways.

Scripture Verses on the Topic

Hebrews 11:6
Ephesians 6:16
1 John 5:4
Romans 4:20-21
Proverbs 3:5-6

Desired Outcome from the Application

We're hoping that a deeper understanding of trusting God by faith and a couple of practical application points come out of this study. As we see through Scripture, this is an essential for the Christian who is hoping to grow closer to God.

Other Helpful Resources

Max Ander's Book, 30 Days to Growing in Your Faith: Enrich Your Life in 15 Minutes a Day is a great addition to any study on this topic.

Optional Scripture Memory Verses

Proverbs 3:5-6

Hebrews 11:6

Week 13

Taming The Tongue

Why is this Topic Important?

An inability to tame the tongue indicates a major weak point in the Christian's life. We read in Ephesians 4 that we should not have any corrupting talk coming out of our mouths, but only talk that builds people up. In James 3, we see an inability to tame the tongue opens us up to all types of unrighteousness, and certainly, as we desire to be salt and light of Christ to those around us, taming the tongue is a first step toward that goal.

Practical Application Points

1. Share with them how you've been able to tame the tongue and seen victory in this area.

2. A Bible study of James 3 would be beneficial, in addition to going through the additional given verses on this topic.

3. If either of you struggle in this area, add that struggle to the ongoing prayer requests between the two of you.

Scripture Verses on the Topic

Ephesians 4:29

Colossians 4:6

James 1:26

James 3:1-12

Desired Outcome from the Application

Because the way we talk can either be such a testimony of our trust and faith in Jesus, this is a really important topic. You're hoping that if your disciplee has had trouble in this area, they see their need to be working on this, both through prayer and encouragement from others to be growing this is area.

Other Helpful Resources

I have often referred people to a wonderful GotQuestions.org article on this topic: https://www.gotquestions.org/taming-the-tongue.html

Optional Scripture Memory Verses

Colossians 4:6

James 1:26

Week 14

Use Of Time

Why is this Topic Important?

The use of our time as Christians is important because our time on earth is limited. How we spend the time God has given us, either for ourselves or for the advancement of His kingdom matters to God.

Practical Application Points

1. Talk through what you think an effective use of our time looks like.

2. Help them create a weekly schedule to make the best use of time.

3. Encourage them to be always looking to make the best use of their time.

Scripture Verses on the Topic

Ephesians 5:15-17

Psalm 90:10-12

Ecclesiastes 3:1

James 4:14

Desired Outcome from the Application

You're hoping to have at least two major outcomes from this study. First, an understanding of how short our time is here on earth and how

God does want us to use it wisely. Secondly, being able to form and keep a schedule that makes the most of the time we have is important as well.

Other Helpful Resources

Helpful Billy Graham online article: https://billygraham.org/story/three-ways-to-use-time-wisely/

Making use of a online or printed calendar can be quite helpful.

Optional Scripture Memory Verses

Ephesians 5:15-16

Colossians 4:5

Week 15

Obedience

Why is this Topic Important?

Obedience in the Christian life is important for a couple of reasons and has a couple of different areas we're asked to be obedient. Both obedience to the Bible and obedience then to both God and Jesus are required. It is a way to both glorify God and show our love and respect for Him. And the call toward obedience is for our benefit. God knows what is best for us and how to grow us to be stronger people and followers of Christ.

Practical Application Points

1. Talk with them about what they think obedience to God is and how we as Christians can obey.

2. Talk with them then about how to apply God's word and the commands of Jesus into our daily lives.

3. Share with them one example of a time in your life you obeyed God and what you saw God do through that time.

Scripture Verses on the Topic

Psalm 119:59-60

John 14:15-21

1 Samuel 15:22

James 4:17

Desired Outcome from the Application

You're hoping that those you disciple are able to read a passage of Scripture and find ways to obey anything they've read, and know how to discern that which requires their obedience. You're also wanting this obedience to come from a love for God and His Son Jesus. As we read in John 14:15, "If you love me, you will keep my commandments."

Other Helpful Resources

A slow, purposeful study of John 14 and 15 would go a long way to further understanding of obedience.

Optional Scripture Memory Verses

John 14:21

James 4:17

Week 16

Discerning The Will Of God

Why is this Topic Important?

It may be obvious why this topic is important: We all want to know God's will for our life and desire to be in His will. But discerning God's will can be hard. It comes through a deepening relationship with Him. I've often pointed people toward Romans 12:1-2, "I appeal to you therefore, brothers, by the mercies of God, to present your bodies as a living sacrifice, holy and acceptable to God, which is your spiritual worship. Do not be conformed to this world, but be transformed by the renewal of your mind, that by testing you may discern what is the will of God, what is good and acceptable and perfect." We see Paul teaching us that it's through surrendering ourselves to God and by renewing our minds in that relationship that we can find God's will.

Practical Application Points

1. Do a study of Romans 12:1-2 together.
2. Share a time that you were seeking God's will and how He showed it to you.
3. Begin a discussion about how they now make decisions in their life and how they can begin seeking God in all decisions.

Scripture Verses on the Topic

Psalm 119:105

Proverbs 15:22

John 16:13

Romans 12:1-2

Desired Outcome from the Application

As you do this study with them, being able to see them begin to make decisions through the lens of Scripture and taking the time to be with God in prayer and supplication as they seek God's will for their lives.

Other Helpful Resources

Bible.org has a wonderful article on this topic that I often refer others to read: https://bible.org/article/discerning-will-god

Optional Scripture Memory Verses

Romans 12:2

Psalm 37:23

Week 17

Being Fruitful For Christ

Why is this Topic Important?

As you read in Chapter 2, being fruitful for Christ is one of my marks of a disciple and is a way we show how we're doing spiritually. The Bible is clear that every good tree is going to bear good fruit and a bad tree will produce bad fruit. In addition, Jesus is clear in Matthew that "every tree therefore that does not bear good fruit is cut down and thrown into the fire." Knowing what fruit is and how to produce good fruit in our lives is really important!

Practical Application Points

1. Read John 15:1-7 together and make application points for both of your lives and make goals around ways to produce good fruit.

2. Talk about how each person is doing in the fruit of the Spirit in Galatians 5 and have each other hold the other person accountable in areas where growth is needed.

Scripture Verses on the Topic

John 15:1-7

Matthew 7:17-20

Luke 6:43-45

Galatians 5:22-23

Desired Outcome from the Application

Being able to distinguish between good fruit and bad fruit in a Christian's life is a great step towards greater spiritual formation. You'll want to make sure that they understand that as Christians, we always want to be producing good fruit and that the fruit of the Spirit is a great guide to how well you're connected to Christ and the Holy Spirit.

Other Helpful Resources

Robby Gallaty's book, Bearing Fruit: What Happens When God's People Grow is a great read for further study.

Optional Scripture Memory Verses

John 15:4

Matthew 7:17-18

Week 18

Satan: Know Your Enemy

Why is this Topic Important?

The Bible is clear that we have an enemy and he is active in the world. 1 Peter tells us that "Your adversary the devil prowls around like a roaring lion, seeking someone to devour." Being able to recognize this enemy and know how to fight effectively against him is important. As I wrote in Chapter 5, with his limited power, he actively works to nullify the effect of the Word of God in people's hearts and he is not happy and will work against you as you begin discipling someone in a discipleship relationship.

Practical Application Points

1. Talk with them about their biggest temptations and share about how you've seen God help you overcome your biggest temptations.

2. Begin actively praying together that God would enable you to overcome the enemy's schemes.

3. Do a Bible study of Ephesians 6:10-18 together.

Scripture Verses on the Topic

Ephesians 6:10-18

1 Peter 5:8-9

John 8:44

John 10:10

Desired Outcome from the Application

You'll want to see them be able to both recognize when Satan is attacking and how to handle that attack through prayer and Scripture. Knowing that, although Satan does have dominion over the world, as Christ followers we have ultimate victory through the finished work of Christ on the cross.

Other Helpful Resources

I've always found Dennis McCallum's book <u>Satan and His Kingdom: What the Bible Says and How It Matters to You</u> a great read for deeper understanding.

Optional Scripture Memory Verses

1 Peter 5:8

John 10:10

Week 19

Dealing With Sin

Why is this Topic Important?

Because we know that all humans are sinful, sin is unfortunately a part of our human existence. Being able to handle that sin and know how to identify sin areas in one's life, to have a plan to have victory in those sin areas is an important topic for you to cover with your disciplee. Being able to find victory as we properly handle sin in our lives, our lives changes, living in the confidence found in being forgiven in Christ. We then can live our lives certain that our past, present, and future sins are as far from us as the East is from the West.

Practical Application Points

1. Talk about our sinful nature and how that seems to manifest in each other's lives. As Jesus says in Mark 14, "The spirit indeed is willing, but the flesh is weak."

2. Share with them how you've seen sin show itself in your life and ways you've seen Jesus provide victory.

3. 1 John 1:9 gives us a great path forward in relation to victory over sin. Talk through this path and how to apply it in our lives.

Scripture Verses on the Topic

Colossians 3:9-10

1 Peter 1:14-16

Romans 13:14

Mark 14:38

1 John 1:8-9

Desired Outcome from the Application

Far too often in our churches, identifying sin in our lives and how to find victory is underplayed. Obviously in your disciple making, you don't want to underplay it. Helping your people identify sin and find victory through Scripture and through Christ is key. Finally, you'll want to underscore how continuing in sin and sinful behavior is dangerous for our lives and our relationship with Christ.

Other Helpful Resources

GotQuestions.org has a great article:

https://www.gotquestions.org/handling-sin.html

Optional Scripture Memory Verses

Psalm 103:12

Romans 13:14

Week 20

Assurance Of Forgiveness

Why is this Topic Important?

1 John 1:9 leads the way for us here, "If we confess our sins, he is faithful and just to forgive us our sins and to cleanse us from all unrighteousness." Living our lives in this truth is important for the growing disciple of Jesus. Far too many people continue to struggle with past sin and it weighs down their life. There is tremendous freedom found in living a life with the knowledge about the forgiveness we have in Christ!

Practical Application Points

1. Talk with them about how they believe they've experienced forgiveness for sin.

2. Share your journey of assurance of forgiveness and how you've seen God forgive you through your relationship with Christ.

Scripture Verses on the Topic

1 John 1:9

Psalm 32:1

Matthew 18:15

Psalm 103:8-12

Desired Outcome from the Application

You want anyone you disciple to be able to live daily in the assurance that they are forgiven for past, present and future sins. This doesn't give us a license to sin, but should rather drive us deeper into our love for Christ, knowing what He has done for us in the area of forgiveness. You also want then them to be able to express to others their confidence that they are forgiven, based on the promises found in God's word.

Other Helpful Resources

Discipleshiplibrary.com has several good resources on this topic. Simply go to the site and type in Assurance of Forgiveness.

Optional Scripture Memory Verses

1 John 1:9

Psalm 32:1

Week 21

Tithing To The Lord's Work

Why is this Topic Important?

While the concept of tithing is from the Old Testament, we see this concept carry over to the New Testament. In the Old Testament, it was a requirement under Old Testament law, while in the New Testament, there is no minimum requirement for how much we should tithe. We do see however certain benefits for contributing to the Lord's work as we go to God and ask Him how much and who to contribute toward. This topic is important both because it is a biblical topic and because certain churches and denominations pervert both the amounts and God's response when we tithe. Having a biblical understanding of this topic is worth the time investment.

Practical Application Points

1. Talk with them about their current tithing understanding and application.
2. Go through the included verses and develop together a 'here's what the Bible says about tithing.'
3. Help them develop a healthy understanding of and application of the verses in relation to tithing.

Scripture Verses on the Topic

2 Chronicles 31:4-5

Mark 12:41-44

1 Corinthians 16:2

2 Corinthians 9:6-7

Desired Outcome from the Application

Being able to understand the Biblical teaching on tithing and having several important organizations they are tithing to based on how they felt God leading them would be a great outcome.

Other Helpful Resources

GotQuestions.org has a helpful article and video here:

https://www.gotquestions.org/tithing-Christian.html

Optional Scripture Memory Verses

2 Corinthians 9:6-7

Mark 12:43-44

Week 22

Biblical Conflict Resolution

Why is this Topic Important?

Biblical conflict resolution is important for a couple of reasons. First, as we gather together as the body of Christ, the Lord wants us to maintain unity with one another. The apostle Paul makes this point clear in Ephesians 4 as he urged us to "walk in a manner worthy of the calling to which you have been called, with all humility and gentleness, with patience, bearing with one another in love, eager to maintain the unity of the Spirit in the bond of peace." Maintaining unity in the body of Christ is important, then, because it enables us to 'walk in a manner worthy of the calling' we've received as believers in Christ. Unity is one of the key ways the Holy Spirit works in our lives. The Holy Spirit enables us to have faith in Christ, bears the fruit of love in our lives and gives us a common trait of caring for one another. Our common convictions and care are from the Holy Spirit, prompting Paul to call it 'the unity of the Spirit.' Secondly, as the secular world watches the church, and us as His disciples, they should observe us resolving conflict in a way that glorifies the Lord, edifies the body of Christ, and reflects the principles laid out in Scripture.

Practical Application Points

1. As you go through the provided Scripture verses, talk about what it looks like to get the 'log out of our eye.'

2. Find the article provided in the Helpful Resources section here on the '4 G's' of Peacemaking and talk through what that would look like for both of you to follow that process every time you needed to go through a Biblical resolution process.

Scripture Verses on the Topic

Matthew 18:15-18

Matthew 7:3-5

Colossians 3:12-15

Ephesians 4:1-3

Desired Outcome from the Application

As I mentioned at the top of this section, Biblical conflict resolution is a way that the outside world sees how we deal with conflict, so a desired outcome would be to make sure that your disciplee has a great grasp of what this looks like Biblically and how to put those principles into practice.

Other Helpful Resources

Ken Sande, the founder and former president of Peacemaker Ministries and the original author of the '4 G's' of Peacemaking has a wonderful webpage on these 4G's: https://rw360.org/the-four-gs/

Optional Scripture Memory Verses

Matthew 7:3

Ephesians 4:1-3

Week 23

Biblically Dealing With Anger

<u>Why is this Topic Important?</u>

There are at least two main reasons that this topic is important: First, in multiple places throughout Scripture, we see that persistent anger is a manifestation of sin in the life of the Christian and we are told to not do it. In fact, in Galatians 5, Paul writes that 'fits of anger' are one of the 'works of the flesh' and one who persists in them 'will not inherit the kingdom of God.' Secondly, one with a persistent anger issue will have a hard time following the admonition of Jesus in Matthew 5 to "let your light shine before others, so that they may see your good works and give glory to your Father who is in heaven."

<u>Practical Application Points</u>

1. Talk with them about how they deal with anger and if they have any 'trouble' areas.

2. Share with them how do handle times you're dealing with anger and how Christ has enabled you to find victory in this area.

Scripture Verses on the Topic

Psalm 37:8-9

James 1:19-20

Colossians 3:8

Ephesians 4:26-27

Desired Outcome from the Application

You'll want to use this time to probe a bit about whether the person you're discipling has any anger issues. The original guy who discipled me told me a story once that early in the discipleship relationship with another, he'd want to take his disciplee to play flag football or golf because he'd be able to see how the disciplee does when others may show frustration and anger. If there are any issues, taking time to deal with them biblically and helping them find victory in the area of anger.

Other Helpful Resources

Robert D. Jones' book Uprooting Anger: Biblical Help for a Common Problem is a great resource for those wanting to go deeper into the causes and ways to find victory over anger.

Optional Scripture Memory Verses

James 1:19-20

Ephesians 4:25-27

Week 24

The Christian's Role In The Great Commission

Why is this Topic Important?

I would define the Great Commission as 'God's plan for building His Church through the preaching of the Gospel, the making of disciples, the confirmation of disciples through both baptism and the ongoing teaching of disciples to be His effective witnesses in our local area and around the world.' This definition is established through several primary Bible passages and a lot of interaction with many Christians who are heavily invested in it's completion. Because these verses, like the aforementioned Matthew 28:18-20 and Acts 1:8 are commands that Jesus gives to His followers, it is germane for all Christians to be obeying these commands.

Practical Application Points

1. Talk about how they perceive Matthew 28:18-20 and where they've seen their place in that work.

2. Walk through where they are feeling led to proclaim the Gospel and make disciples. This could be in their local area or some place around the world. Pray together for where they are feeling led.

3. As a way to understand the needs of the Global Lost, visit JoshuaProject.net and talk together about the stats around how many worldwide still have not heard the Gospel.

Scripture Verses on the Topic

Matthew 28:18-20

Matthew 24:14

Acts 1:8

John 20:21

Desired Outcome from the Application

Because the Great Commission is the call of Christ to 'Go make disciples' and 'Go proclaim the Gospel,' and that these commands are from Christ and are for all Christians, finding one's place in that work is important. The pioneer English missionary to China, Hudson Taylor said of the Great Commission that "The Great Commission is not an option to be considered; it is a command to be obeyed." You're looking from your disciplee a growing understanding of the call of the Great Commission and a growing obedience toward it's completion.

Other Helpful Resources

The Joshua Project website has a vast wealth of information about the people groups of the world that are not yet reached. Taking some time at JoshuaProject.net to investigate where the Gospel has not yet gone would add to your understanding and teaching of this topic.

In addition, a simple YouTube search for Great Commission will yield many great video teaching resources to understand the topic even better.

Optional Scripture Memory Verses

Matthew 28:18-20

Mark 16:15

How To Begin Memorizing Scripture

As you have read in this book a couple of times, I have been a longtime proponent of the spiritual discipline of Scripture memorization. Dallas Willard, former Professor of Philosophy at the University of Southern California and prolific author on spiritual growth wrote, "Bible memorization is absolutely fundamental to spiritual formation. If I had to choose between all the disciplines of the spiritual life, I would choose Bible memorization, because it is a fundamental way of filling our minds with what it needs. This book of the law shall not depart out of your mouth. That's where you need it! How does it get in your mouth? Memorization."[1] As you begin your discipleship ministry, I strongly recommend that you encourage those you are discipling to memorize the two verses every week that I've given you that correspond with the weekly topic. It really is just a great 'add on' to your lesson and will help them as they learn the truths found in God's word found in each weekly topic.

Here are a couple of keys to Bible memorization: First, teaching your people to memorize each passage in a particular way is an important and helpful tool. As I have memorized scripture verses, I always memorize the title first, then the reference, then the verse, then I say the reference again.

---

1. "Spiritual Formation in Christ for the Whole Life and Whole Person" in Vocatio, Vol. 12, no. 2, Spring, 2001, p. 7

Here is an example:

Scripture Memory (title)

Joshua 1:8 (reference)

"This Book of the Law shall not depart from your mouth, but you shall meditate on it day and night, so that you may be careful to do according to all that is written in it. For then you will make your way prosperous, and then you will have good success." (the Bible verse)

Joshua 1:8 (repeat the reference again)

If you and disciplees say each of these parts in this order, you will find it helpful because not only will you memorize the verse, but the title acts as the 'handle' that will help you retrieve the verse that you've memorized when you need to recall it. For the Scripture verses recommended for memorization for each weekly topic, just use the title for each weekly topic that corresponds with the verse. (Use the example above for a reference.)

The final step for successful Scripture memorization is having a 'Scripture Memory Buddy' to both help keep you accountable and to quiz you on the verses as you memorize them. This could be a spouse, friend or accountability partner, or in your case, the person/people you are discipling. Having someone in your life whom you know is going to ask you to repeat them from memory is very helpful!

There are a couple of apps for smartphones that are very helpful in memorizing Scripture. The one I like is called *Bible Memory: Remember Me*. While 'back in the day' we would write our Scripture memory verses on cards and have a hard holder that would keep our cards organized, now with apps like Remember Me, you can memorize them in several different ways, and can move them from 'new' to 'due' to 'known' and as you are memorizing the verses, the app will help you memorize them several different ways. There is even a web interface that you can enter the verses from a PC or Mac, and they sync automatically with the app. It can be found on the Apple or Android app stores. For those interested in a card-based system, you can find the original Navigators' Topical Memory System, which has pre-printed cards and a card holder included in the box on Amazon.com.

Scripture Memory as a Part of the 24 Weekly Topics

As you've probably seen, I've given you two Scripture verses to memorize for each of the 24 weekly topics. I would highly recommend that you add time to quiz each other as you memorize these verses, which will only add to everyone's understanding of the topics.

Spiritual Disciplines List

Spiritual disciplines, as I wrote about in Chapter 2, are practices found in Scripture that promote spiritual growth and formation among believers in the gospel of Jesus Christ. They are habits of experiential Christianity and devotion, that have been practiced by God's people since biblical times. These spiritual disciplines are primarily used to aid and guide our growth toward maturity and therefore are to be executed in our lives on a regular basis. Here is my list of 10 spiritual disciplines, together with a brief definition:

Bible Reading

This may be redundant to review, given that one of my six Marks of a Disciples is that the disciple is obedient to the Bible, but it is essential that the disciple of Jesus is spending time daily in God's word. Simply put, if you want to know God and His Son Jesus better, God has given us, in written form, the perfect way to study what it means to know Jesus and know what He's asking us to do. Being a follower of Jesus is about being friends with Jesus. It constitutes a real relationship just like the one you have with your best friend or spouse. In all relationships we talk and we listen to each other. And this is what reading the Bible and praying is all about. When we read the Bible, we are listening to what God has to say to us (except it is written down like in a letter). In the Bible, God has made sure he has told us everything we need to know in order to be the best of friends with him. So when you pray and read, you are really having a good old conversation with God and that is definitely something worth doing every day! In addition, when we read the Bible daily, we can begin to stop doing the things God doesn't want us to do and start becoming more like Jesus everyday, which should be the goal of every Christian.

Prayer

Prayer is simply talking to God, a joining of our soul with God, talking with Him directly. It can take on many forms. It is a 'beseeching of the Lord,' 'pouring out the soul before the Lord', 'praying and crying before the Lord,' a drawing near to God. Prayer requires a belief in the personality of God, his ability and willingness to give us that time with Him, and a belief in His sovereignty, His control of all things. Acceptable prayer must be sincere, offered with reverence and godly fear, with a humble sense of our own insignificance as creatures. As the apostle Paul writes, "do not be anxious about anything, but in everything by prayer and supplication with thanksgiving let your requests be made known to God. And the peace of God, which surpasses all understanding, will guard your hearts and your minds in Christ Jesus."[1]

As you pray, the purpose of prayer is to get right with God and seek His protection again the enemy, to deeper our relationship with him and to pray for those who have not yet accepted Christ.

---

1. Philippians 4:6-7

Scripture Memory

Scripture memory is one of my favorite spiritual disciplines in terms of how God has used it in my life. This is the memorization and mental retention of portions of Scripture that you remember 'by heart.' In my own life, God has used Scripture memory in a number of key ways: It has helped my conform to Christ, I've seen daily triumph over sin and it's a wonderful way to minister to others. As situations arise, to be able to call up Scripture, either in my own battle with a sin issue or as I encourage and minister to others, to have God's word 'hidden in my heart,' it's a wonderful Spiritual discipline to implement into your life. As David wrote in Psalm 119, "I have stored up your word in my heart, that I might not sin against you."[2]

In the resources section of this book, I've included a 'how-to' begin memorizing Scripture. Enjoy!

Worship

As a spiritual discipline, worship should be done daily because of who God is. As the holy and almighty God, the Creator and Sustainer of the universe, the Sovereign Judge to whom we must give an account, He is worthy of all the praise and honor we can give Him. As Donald S. Whitney states, "To worship God means to ascribe the proper worth to God, to magnify His worthiness of praise, or better to approach and address God as He is worthy."[3] John praise God as worthy in Revelation 4 as he states, "Worthy are you, our Lord and God, to receive glory and honor and power, for you created all things, and by your will they existed and were created."[4] While worship often includes actions and words, it is actually being

---

2. Psalm 119:11
3. Donald S. Whitney, Spiritual Disciplines for the Christian Life (Nav Press: Colorado Springs, 2014) p. 103-104
4. Revelation 4:11

preoccupied with God. It is worship that comes from the mind and the heart: a God-centered response of the mind and heart.

Evangelism

As a part of Jesus' ministry, He gave His followers 50 commands for us to follow. We find one of those commands in Mark 16 as Jesus is appearing to people after the resurrection. He commands his followers to, "Go into all the world and proclaim the gospel to the whole creation." As we recall what God has done in our lives through Christ, the disciple of Jesus is honored to maintain the discipline of a rhythm in their lives of intentional witness through evangelism. This sharing of the good news that Jesus came into the world to save the world through Him should be a part of our basic identity as disciples of Jesus. From the days of the early church in Acts until today, we are God's plan A for reaching the world for Christ and there is no plan B. Evangelism is considered a spiritual disciples at least in part because as disciples of Jesus, we should be making time to be sharing the Gospel on a regular basis.

Fasting

Biblical Fasting is the abstinence from food or drink for an extended period for the sake of some spiritual purpose. Almost always, fasting is combined with prayer, and is used to cast off any additional distractions to hear more clearly from God. Many times, fasting is done when one wants to go to God and seek clarity about a particular person, situation, or topic. Fasting can be for one meal or several days, but it's almost always used as a way to hear from God and get clarity on a particular situation.

---

5. Mark 16:15

Journaling

The Spiritual disciple of Journaling is simply the discipline of adding a journal to your times alone with God and recording what comes about in those times. One of the things I love about journaling is that you can make it whatever you'd like to. For some, recording Scripture passages that come to mind, and having them in their journal to recall later is important. For others, praying to God through the written word and recording the answers God is giving back is super beneficial. Journaling has the appeal of combining the motions of our lives with the mind of God. Saturated with prayer, and permeated with God's word, it can be a powerful way to hear from God.

Serving

Spiritual disciplines are practices found in Scripture that promote spiritual growth and formation among believers in the gospel of Jesus Christ, and serving others is a spiritual discipline that definitely can promote spiritual growth. Just the nature of serving requires us to die to our selves and look after the needs of others. As we serve others, taking in the many menial tasks that it often requires, means disciplining ourselves to overcome sloth and pride. We must battle our flesh in order to accomplish it, which it what in part makes it such a great spiritual discipline. This is especially true for those of us who'd like to be in a leadership position. Jesus tell us that "But whoever would be great among you must be your servant, and whoever would be first among you must be your slave, even as the Son of Man came not to be served but to serve, and to give his life as a ransom for many."[6]

---

6. Mark 10:43-45

Stewardship

This spiritual discipline is not one that we hear much about in our churches. But this is the spiritual discipline of a disciplined use of time and money, those things that God has given to us for the purpose of godliness. The apostle Paul encourages us to "Look carefully then how you walk, not as unwise but as wise, making the best use of the time, because the days are evil. Therefore do not be foolish, but understand what the will of the Lord is."[7] Because we have only been given so many days, it's a disciplined process to make wise use of our time. As we all know, our days on earth are short and we want to make sure that we use those days God gives us well.

A disciplined use of the financial resources God gives us a similar discipline. There is a surprising amount of Scripture that addresses the use of wealth and possessions. Paul addresses those who, either through financial irresponsibility or in being lazy, do not provide for those in their own household, "But if anyone does not provide for his relatives, and especially for members of his household, he has denied the faith and is worse than an unbeliever."[8] To the degree that we as Christians use our money accordingly, we show our growth in Christlikeness.

Silence and Solitude

The discipline of silence and solitude is a way for the Christian to temporarily stop speaking in order to either quietly read the Bible, or be in prayer, or both. Although this would include no speaking, praying to God, either silently or out loud, may still occur. In the resources section of this book, I have a worksheet on what I've often called a Time Alone with God (TAWG), which incorporates the spiritual disciple of silence and solitude within it. The purpose of this spiritual discipline is toward the advancement of spiritual purposes. The withdrawing in solitude and the quiet of the silence many times allow the

---

7. Ephesians 5:15-17
8. 1 Timothy 5:8

participant to hear from God where otherwise it may not be possible. I've often said of my extended times alone with God that the first hour or so of Bible reading and prayer is for me just to clear my head of all the 'noise,' with all the busy thoughts and things I have to get done. It's beyond this first hour that I actually begin to hear from God in prayer and Bible reading. Jesus is our best example of this spiritual discipline. He is often retreating to get some silent time alone with God. In Luke 5, for example, as the crowds were gathering and things were happening, "he would withdraw to desolate places and pray."[9]

Perseverance in the Disciplines

After listing these spiritual disciplines, there is one more than requires our attention, which is simply the perseverance to continue in the other nine disciplines. This perseverance can be challenging at times because, as I've mentioned earlier in this book, most of us are quite busy and finding the time to pray, to be memorizing and reading Scripture and finding time to have extended times alone in solitude and silence before the Lord can be hard. This is why the perseverance of these other disciplines is a discipline of its own. Through the power of the Holy Spirit, we can persevere. In fact, we desperately need the Holy Spirit's help with these other disciplines. While some may try to have the discipline to work at them in their lives, it is not possible to increase one's spirituality through these disciplines without the Holy Spirit. We also need each other to successfully practice the spiritual disciplines. As I've mentioned a number of times in this book, we need each other to be providing accountability and encouragement toward our own spiritual growth. John illustrates this well in 1 John 1, "the life was made manifest, and we have seen it, and testify to it and proclaim to you the eternal life, which was with the Father and was made manifest to us— that which we have seen and heard we

---

9. Luke 5:16 |

proclaim also to you, so that you too may have fellowship with us; and indeed our fellowship is with the Father and with his Son Jesus Christ."[10] The victory over those who in our lives oppose the spiritual disciplines is found as we, through the Holy Spirit, and with the encouragement and accountability with others, continually practice and work at the spiritual disciplines.

10. 1 John 1:2-3

Extended Time Alone With God (TAWG)

Almost every Friday that I'm in town, usually from 9AM until about noon, I invest some extended time with God at my favorite outdoor location near my house. I've been purposefully setting aside this time for years and I find it to be a very valuable investment of my time. For many, the idea of this much extended time in prayer can seem so difficult that they never get to it! But this extended time with the Lord is one of the best investments of your time that you can ever make!

This Time Alone with God, or as I like to call it, TAWG, is in addition to your Quiet Times that you spend daily with the Lord. The biggest benefit that I find in these extended periods of time is that it really gives you additional time to praise God and to then hear from Him. I often tell people that I need the first hour to just clear my head of all the distractions: stuff going on at home, on my job, in my marriage, with my kids, etc. Once my mind is cleared, I still have an hour or two to really commune with the Lord and begin to hear clear direction from Him. Here are some highlights of how you can begin adding a TAWG to your schedule, and some step-by-step directions on how to make it work.

Finding a Place to Go

Finding an outdoor setting has worked incredibly well for me, so if you can, I highly recommend that you find an outdoor location for your extended time with the Lord. (Here in Colorado, sometimes an outdoor location doesn't work well, especially in the winter. In those times, I huddle in my basement office!)

Here are a couple of keys for your search: Finding a place where you can be as uninterrupted as possible is a good rule of thumb. Also, there's just something 'magic' about being outside! In the place where I like to go, I can see the Front Range of the Rocky Mountains just west of Denver, and as I am praying and reading Scripture, I can sense and feel God in powerful ways. I often say to the Lord as I'm looking out at the mountains, 'Lord, if you created all of this, and I know You did, anything I bring to You, I am confident You can handle!'

How to Invest your Time

This extended time with God is a great opportunity to connect with God and hear from Him. Let's assume that you decide to dedicate three hours to this time with God, as I often do. You can divide your time between reading Scripture, meditating on the Scripture you read, praying to God and dedicating some time to just being silent before God to hear from Him. While you certainly don't have to do this in just the same way that I do, a good first step would be to split the time into thirds. For the first third of the time, read and pray through Scripture of your choosing. For the second third, invest time praying to the Lord, and for the final third, dedicate that remaining time to hear from God, being silent before the Lord and hearing from Him.

If you may have never 'heard' from God or know how that may occur, please allow me to try to describe briefly how that normally happens.

While God can speak to us in a myriad of ways, such as through angels, visions or miraculous events, you will generally find that God will speak to you through your thoughts. He will use times when you are reading the Bible, praying quietly, or seeking counsel from other Christians as you talk to them about a situation you're trying to figure out.

Here is an example of "hearing from God" that happened in my own life recently. A couple of years ago, I was sensing that perhaps God was asking me to lead our ministry in a different direction. We were doing Bible distribution events in China and I loved the work. As we began to have difficulty finding places to go to distribute Bibles to Christians in rural China where Bibles are not readily accessible, I began asking the Lord what His will was for next steps. As I invested extended time with Him, a deep heart for the people groups around the world that had never heard about Jesus began to well up in my mind. I began to see the passages of Scripture that talk about God's plan for the nations in a new way, and I heard God's 'still, small voice' in my head. I also began to 'run into' people who were doing this work and after hearing of the over 4,000 people groups not yet reached for the Gospel from them, I knew God was leading us to contribute to this need.

After you have some experience doing this exercise, you will find the rhythm and flow that works best for you.

What to take with you

There are a few 'must have' items that you will want to have with you: Bible, paper, and a pen or pencil. Other helpful items might include:

- A favorite devotional book
- Your current prayer list

- Your quiet time journal (or an empty journal for you to begin one!)
- Scripture memory cards
- Notes from your last extended time in prayer

How to stay awake and alert

- Get adequate rest the night before.
- Change positions—sit a while, walk around, sit, walk, and repeat.
- Create variety in what you do. Read the Scriptures, then pray, then write, and so on.
- Pray aloud—in a whisper or soft voice if necessary. For those who love to worship God with music, having a playlist of worship songs on your smartphone may help keep you focused!

Taking notes

Taking notes during your extended time with God will give you a record of the thoughts and words the Lord is speaking to you, as well as helping you keep your time organized.

In addition, when we pray, we often have something come to mind that we feel we should take action on, or that we have forgotten to do—perhaps totally unrelated to what we are praying about. By keeping paper or your device ready to list these things, we can avoid prolonged distraction and then act on them later.

Toward the end of your time in prayer, you will want to spend a few minutes writing down some conclusions. Summarize the major impressions of your time. Keep these notes in a notebook and review them weekly for a while. This will ensure that you follow through on the concepts, commands, or ideas that God has impressed upon you.

A Couple of Closing Thoughts

Lorne Sanny was discipled by The Navigators' founder Dawson Trotman and served as The Navigators General Director for thirty years. I close this resource with a couple of encouraging quotes from him on spending extended time with God.

"The result of your day in prayer should be answers to the two questions Paul asked the Lord on the Damascus road (Acts 22:6-10). Paul's first question was, 'Who are you, Lord?' The Lord replied, 'I am Jesus.' You will be seeking to know Him, to find out who He is. The second question Paul asked was, 'What shall I do, Lord?' and the Lord answered him specifically. This should be answered or reconfirmed for you in that part of the day when you unhurriedly seek His will for you."

"Don't think you must end the day with some new discovery or extraordinary experience. Wait on God and expose yourself to His Word. Looking for a new experience or insight you can share with someone when you get back will get you off the track. True, you may gain some new insight, but often this can just take your attention from the real business. The test of such a day is not how exhilarated we are when the day is over but how it works into life tomorrow. If we have really exposed ourselves to the Word and come into contact with God, it will affect our daily life. God bless you as you do this—and do it soon!"[1]

---

1. https://www.navigators.org/resource/spend-extended-time-prayer/

The 50 Commands Of Jesus

As Christians, we should know the commands of Christ and obey them. Jesus Himself says in John 14:21, **"Whoever has my commandments and keeps them, he it is who loves me. And he who loves me will be loved by my Father, and I will love him and manifest myself to him."** What makes something that Jesus said a command? Taking the dictionary definition of Command: to direct authoritatively or to order. In the case of Jesus' commands, they are definitive statements where He's telling us authoritatively to do something. Use this included resource as a Bible Study you can go through together with those you are discipling to know the commands of Jesus in order to begin obeying them. Simply take one command each week and do the study to help you know each command.

1. Read the Command in the Bible, reading the paragraph before and after
2. Find one way to obey the command in light of John 14:21
3. Tell someone about what you've learned

1. Repent - Matthew 4:17

2. Follow Me - Matthew 4:19

3. Rejoice - Matthew 5:12

4. Let Your Light Shine - Matthew 5:16

5. Be Reconciled - Matthew 5:24-25

6. Do Not Lust – Matthew 5:29-30

7. Keep Your Word - Matthew 5:37

8. Go the Second Mile - Matthew 5:38-42

9. Love Your Enemies - Matthew 5:44

10. Be Perfect - Matthew 5:48

11. Practice Spiritual Disciplines in Secret– Matthew 6:1-18

12. Lay Up Treasures - Matthew 6:19-21

13. Seek God's Kingdom - Matthew 6:33

14. Judge Not - Matthew 7:1

15. Do Not Cast Pearls - Matthew 7:6

16. Ask, Seek, and Knock - Matthew 7:7-8

17. Do Unto Others - Matthew 7:12

18. Choose the Narrow Way – Matthew 7:13-14

19. Beware of False Prophets – Matthew 7:15

20. Pray For Laborers - Matthew 9:38

21. Be Wise as Serpents - Matthew 10:16

22. Fear Not - Matthew 10:26

23. Hear God's Voice - Matthew 11:15

24. Come to Me and Take My Yoke - Matthew 11:28-29

25. Honor Your Parents - Matthew 15:4

26. Beware of Leaven - Matthew 16:6

27. Despise Not Little Ones – Matthew 18:10

28. Go To Offenders - Matthew 18:15

29. Forgive Offenders - Matthew 18:21-22

30. Honor Marriage - Matthew 19:6

31. Be a Servant - Matthew 20:26-28

32. Be a House of Prayer - Matthew 21:13

33. Ask in Faith - Matthew 21:21-22

34. Render to Caesar - Matthew 22:19-21

35. Love the Lord with Everything - Matthew 22:37-38

36. Love Your Neighbor - Matthew 22:39

37. Await My Return - Matthew 24:42-44

38. Take, Eat, and Drink – Matthew 26:26-27

39. Watch and Pray - Matthew 26:41

40. Baptize and Teach My Disciples - Matthew 28:19

41. Make Disciples - Matthew 28:19

42. Go Proclaim the Gospel - Mark 16:15

43. Deny Yourself - Luke 9:23

44. Beware of Covetousness - Luke 12:15

45. Do Not Be Anxious about your Life – Luke 12:22

46. Bring in the Poor - Luke 14:12-14

47. Receive God's Power - Luke 24:49

48. Be Born Again - John 3:7

49. Keep My Commandments - John 14:15

Notes

<u>Notes</u>

Made in USA - North Chelmsford, MA
1334973_9781733628358
09.28.2022 1430